SAVORY BITES FROM YOUR CAKE POP MAKER

75 Fun Snacks, Adorable Appetizers & Delicious Entrees

Heather Torrone

Ulysses Press

Published by:
Ulysses Press
P.O. Box 3440
Berkeley, CA 94703
www.ulyssespress.com

ISBN: 978-1-61243-175-8
Library of Congress Catalog Number 2013931802

Printed in the United States by Bang Printing

10 9 8 7 6 5 4 3 2 1

Acquisitions editor: Kelly Reed
Managing editor: Claire Chun
Editor: Lauren Harrison
Proofreader: Elyce Berrigan-Dunlop
Production: what!design @ whatweb.com
Index: Sayre Van Young
Cover design: what!design @ whatweb.com
Photographs: © www.judiswinksphotography.com
Stylist for featured recipes: Anna Hartman-Kenzler

Distributed by Publishers Group West

TABLE OF CONTENTS

BEEF, PORK, AND LAMB 41

INTRODUCTION

I grew up in a family of five girls, and we all had our fair share of playing "kitchen." My sisters and I would mix things together from the refrigerator and dare each other to "try it." After many years of being the one who had no problem trying anything, I developed a keen sense for what ingredients go well together, and which are just plain gross. With *Savory Bites from Your Cake Pop Maker*, I hope you enjoy "trying it," too.

My obsession with these delicious morsels comes from their amazing ability to make meals into glorious, bite-size gastronomic explosions. And cooking in the cake pop maker is so fun and easy! Recipes cook in only a few short minutes, allowing you to serve delicious and simple dishes with relatively little effort. Savory bites combine all the best fresh, wholesome ingredients into tasty appetizers, breakfasts, and lunches. You can use ingredients most likely already in your fridge to quickly make the most impressive school lunches, tastiest breakfasts, and delicious last-minute nibbles for any surprise guests. They're the perfect way to feed a few individuals or a large number of guests with as little in the way of serve ware as a napkin. When you're cooking for a crowd, using a cake pop maker allows you to enjoy more of the party and spend less time preparing in the kitchen during your event.

These recipes reflect where I live, which is in a diverse community with an abundance of different ethnic dishes. It dawned on me while thinking of my favorite recipes that a majority of people may not have the same influences as I do. I'm so excited to introduce a little of what I've experienced, tasted, and found to be delicious with many others.

The recipes in this book use all types of dough. Some are as simple as cutting store bought biscuits in half, and some require combining a few simple ingredients from your pantry. The dough is generally divided before you begin assembling the pops. This allows your pops to be consistent in size and helps to keep the proportions manageable.

There are some great tools I recommend having on hand to help you make your pops quickly and easily:

- A mini rolling pin to stretch out your dough pieces. They are sold at most craft stores or online. I have even borrowed my daughter's Play-Doh rolling pin from time to time.

- A couple flexible plastic cutting mats, usually sold in sets of three. They are worth it! I roll all my dough on them, and clean-up takes seconds since they go right in the dishwasher.

- A plastic mini ruler will help you make sure your dough and food pieces are consistently the right size.

- A 1¼-tablespoon-size cookie scoop. This will help you scoop ingredients right from the mixing bowl into the cake pop maker with as little work as possible.

- The fork tool that's included with most cake pop makers is used to gently remove bites from the appliance.

- Parchment paper is great to wrap any unused dough in and it is instrumental in preparing burgers, like those on page 42.

- Spray oil is a must to have on hand for many recipes (although some do not require it). I prefer to use organic sunflower oil to grease the wells of the cake pop maker, but you can also use vegetable oil spray. I often use organic olive oil spray as well.

- Paper towels are essential for cleaning your cake pop maker, which may seem a bit overwhelming after cooking some of the greasier recipes in this book. However, if you blot any excess fat with a paper towel while the cake pop maker is still hot and then wait until the appliance has cooled completely, it's not so hard to get those little bits off.

I hope you enjoy cooking from this book as much as I enjoyed working on these mini bites of perfection. The recipes are so good they'll make you stop whatever you are doing and start cooking!

BREAKFAST

FRENCH TOAST

This is a great recipe to get the kids involved. It's not only fun, but easy! Be careful about how tightly you squeeze the bread into a ball. Too loose of a ball will result in a messy pop. Too tight of a ball will make a pop that's not full and perfectly round. *Makes 12 pops*

2 large eggs

1 tablespoon milk

¼ teaspoon vanilla extract

6 slices bread

¼ cup (½ stick) sweet cream butter, at room temperature

¼ cup sugar

1 teaspoon ground cinnamon, or to taste

maple syrup or powdered sugar, to serve

1. Break the eggs into a small bowl, add the milk and vanilla, and whisk to combine. Cut all the crusts off the bread slices. Spread a little butter on half of each bread slice. Sprinkle the buttered portion of bread with sugar, and the entire slice of bread lightly with cinnamon. Cut the bread slices in half, for a total of 12 pieces that are each one-half butter sugar, and cinnamon, and one-half cinnamon only. Roll each bread strip into a ball and gently squeeze together.

2. Dip the balls into the egg and milk mixture. When the cake pop maker is hot, place 1 ball into each well. Cook for 4 minutes, until golden brown. Serve with maple syrup or sprinkle with powdered sugar.

VARIATIONS: Substitute the butter, cinnamon, and sugar for: ½ tablespoon cream cheese and 1 teaspoon strawberry jam; or ½ tablespoon peanut butter and 1 teaspoon Nutella.

VEGETABLE EGG STRATA

Makes 24 pops

4 large eggs

1/3 cup half-and-half

4 slices white sandwich bread, cubed

1/3 cup diced red bell pepper

1/3 cup diced zucchini

1/4 cup diced sweet white onion

1 cup shredded mozzarella cheese

salt and pepper

1. Crack the eggs into a medium bowl, add the half-and-half, and whisk to combine. Then add the bread cubes, red pepper, zucchini, onion, and mozzarella cheese. Season with salt and pepper. Mix all the ingredients together.

2. When the cake pop maker is hot, spray with olive oil. Fill each well with ¾ tablespoon of the mixture. Cook for 4 minutes, until lightly golden. Repeat with the remaining egg mixture.

BAKED APPLE AND RAISIN OATMEAL POPS

These are great for breakfast or lunch on the go. I love them made with Honeycrisp apples. *Makes 30 pops*

1½ cups old-fashioned oats

¼ cup light brown sugar, lightly packed

½ cup all-purpose flour

1 teaspoon baking powder

½ teaspoon salt

1 teaspoon ground cinnamon

¼ cup honey

2 eggs

½ cup whole milk

1 teaspoon vanilla extract

½ cup raisins

½ cup diced, peeled apple

1. Place all the ingredients except the raisins and apple in a medium bowl and stir to combine well. Then add the raisins and diced apple and stir to combine.

2. When the cake pop maker is hot, spray with sunflower or vegetable oil. Fill each well with about 1 tablespoon batter. Cook for 4 minutes, until medium-dark golden. Serve warm.

VEGETARIAN BRUNCH POPS

Makes 20 pops

1 medium Chinese eggplant, diced

1 medium red bell pepper, diced

1 jalapeño pepper, seeded and diced (optional)

1 (7.5-ounce) tube home-style biscuits

fresh basil leaves

4 ounces cream cheese, cut into ½-inch cubes

salt and pepper

1. Set a large skillet over medium heat and spray with olive oil. When the pan is hot, add the eggplant, red pepper, and jalapeño pepper, if using, and sauté until softened, about 9 minutes. Season with salt and pepper. Let cool.

2. Separate the biscuits, cut each one in half for a total of 20, and flatten with your thumbs. Put half a basil leaf and a cube of cream cheese in the center of each biscuit half, and then spoon 1 tablespoon eggplant and pepper mixture on top. Pinch the sides together over the filling to seal each half-biscuit into a ball.

3. When the cake pop maker is hot, spray with sunflower or vegetable oil. Place 1 dough ball in each well and cook for 3 minutes, until golden brown.

PANCAKE POPS

This batter is plentiful and freezes well. I make these on Saturday mornings and use the leftover batter all week long. I make a different variation every week, but my family really likes strawberry cream cheese pancake bites the best (see recipe below)!   *Makes 50 pops*

1¾ cups all-purpose flour

2 teaspoons baking powder

½ teaspoon baking soda

¼ teaspoon kosher salt

2 teaspoons ground cinnamon

1⅓ cups milk

1 large egg

¼ cup honey

2 tablespoons unsalted butter, melted

maple syrup, to serve

1. In a large bowl, whisk together the flour, baking powder, baking soda, salt, and cinnamon. Add the milk, egg, honey, and melted butter, and whisk until smooth.

2. When the cake pop maker is hot, spray with sunflower or vegetable oil. Fill each well with ¾ tablespoon batter. Cook for 3 minutes, until medium brown. Serve with maple syrup. Store any leftover batter in zip-top bags in the freezer for up to 1 week.

STRAWBERRY CREAM CHEESE: Buy strawberry cream cheese from a deli, bagel store, or grocery store and fill a sandwich-size zip-top bag with about 1 cup cream cheese. Make a small cut in 1 bottom corner of the bag, then squeeze ¼ teaspoon cream cheese into the batter-filled wells of a cake pop maker before cooking.

PIGGIE CAKES: Buy breakfast sausage and cook according to the package directions. Insert a 1-inch section of the cooked sausage into the batter-filled wells of the cake pop maker before cooking. When the cooked pancake bites are still hot, insert a lollipop stick into the sausage end of each pop and allow to cool. Your kids will think you're a rock star!

EGGS BENEDICT

These are great when serving brunch at a party.   *Makes 24 pops*

4 slices Canadian bacon

6 medium hard-boiled eggs

1 recipe Savory Bites Bread Dough (page 91)

1 cup (2 sticks) sweet cream butter

4 large egg yolks

1 teaspoon Dijon mustard

2 tablespoons fresh lemon juice

salt and pepper

1. Cook the Canadian bacon according to directions on package. Then divide each slice of bacon into about 1-inch squares. I got 12 squares from each slice. Cut each hard-boiled egg in half vertically and then diagonally. This will give you 4 wedges per egg. Roll out each dough square so it's 3 to 4 inches.

2. In microwave-safe bowl, microwave the butter to melt completely. In a blender on high speed, combine the egg yolks, mustard, and lemon juice. Then, with the blender running, stream the hot melted butter into the blender and purée for 2 minutes. This will produce a thick, creamy, yellow sauce. Season with salt and pepper.

3. On each rolled-out dough square, place a square of Canadian bacon, ¼ teaspoon of the creamy sauce, then 1 egg wedge. Pinch opposite ends of dough over the filling and shape into a ball. Repeat with the remaining ingredients.

4. When the cake pop maker is hot, spray with sunflower or vegetable oil. Place 1 dough ball in each well and cook for 2 to 3 minutes, until light golden brown.

CHOCOLATE CROISSANTS

Makes 24 pops

1 (8-ounce) tube seamless crescent dough

8 mini snack size Hershey's chocolate bars

powdered sugar, for sprinkling

1. Roll out the crescent dough and cut into 16 (3 x 3-inch) squares. Using a mini rolling pin, roll out each square to about 3 inches and fill with 2 squares of chocolate. If you stack the 2 squares on top of one another, this will make it easier to close the pop. Pinch opposite ends of the dough closed over the chocolate squares and form into balls.

2. When the cake pop maker is hot, place 1 dough ball in each well and cook for 3 minutes, until golden brown. Let cool for 5 minutes and then sprinkle with powdered sugar.

CHOCOLATE CROISSANTS

POULTRY AND SEAFOOD

BUFFALO BALLS

Makes 24 pops

2 large boneless, skinless chicken breasts (about 1½ pounds total)

¼ cup hot sauce

6 ounces cream cheese, softened

2 ounces blue cheese

1 (8-ounce) tube seamless crescent dough

salt and pepper

ranch dressing or blue cheese dressing, to serve

1. Spray a medium sauté pan or skillet with olive oil and warm over medium heat. Place the chicken breasts over medium heat and cook for about 8 minutes total, flipping the chicken over halfway through. While cooking, season with salt, pepper, and hot sauce. When the chicken is cooked through, shred it into small pieces and transfer to a medium bowl to cool. Add the cream cheese and blue cheese to the chicken, and stir to combine.

2. Roll out the crescent dough and divide into 24 (2-inch) squares. Use a mini rolling pin to roll out each square so it's 3 to 4 inches. Add a little less than a 1-tablespoon-size scoop of chicken and cheese mixture onto each square. Pinch the ends of the dough together over the filling to form a ball.

3. When the cake pop maker is hot, place 1 dough ball in each well. Cook for 3 minutes, until golden brown. Let cool for a couple minutes before serving with ranch or blue cheese dressing for dipping.

CHICKEN COBB SANDWICHES

Makes 24 pops

½ pound boneless, skinless chicken breast, grilled and diced

2 large hard-boiled eggs, diced

½ medium to large tomato, diced

½ avocado, diced

4 slices bacon, cooked and crumbled

pinch of salt

1 tablespoon crumbled blue cheese

1 recipe Savory Bites Bread Dough (page 91)

½ cup Thousand Island dressing, to serve

1. In a medium bowl, gently combine the chicken, eggs, tomato, avocado, bacon, salt, and blue cheese.

2. Roll out the dough and divide into 24 (2-inch squares). Roll out the dough squares with a mini rolling pin so each square is 3 to 4 inches. Scoop a generous ½-tablespoon portion of chicken mixture onto each square. Close the dough over the chicken mixture and pinch closed.

3. When the cake pop maker is hot, spray with sunflower or vegetable oil. Place 1 dough ball in each well and cook for 2 minutes, until a light golden brown. Serve at room temperature with Thousand Island dressing.

CHICKEN PARMESAN BITES

These little nuggets are great to feed a group of kids or adults. For a little extra zing, add a small piece of roasted pepper to each pop along with the mozzarella.

Makes 36 pops

2 large boneless, skinless chicken breasts (about 1½ pounds total)

4 ounces mozzarella cheese

2 large eggs

1 tablespoon whole milk

1 cup grated Parmesan cheese

2 cups Italian-style breadcrumbs

marinara red sauce, for dipping

1. Cut the chicken into 1-inch squares. Cut the mozzarella cheese into ½ x ¼-inch pieces. Make a small slit into the center of each chicken cube, and insert a piece of the cheese.

2. In a small bowl, beat the eggs with the milk. On a large plate, combine the Parmesan cheese and the breadcrumbs. A few pieces at a time, bathe the cheese-filled chicken cubes in the eggs and then coat them with the breadcrumb mixture. Repeat until all the chicken pieces are coated.

3. When the cake pop maker is hot, spray with olive oil. Place a chicken piece in each of about 8 wells at a time and cook for 4½ minutes, until cooked through. Be sure to open 1 bite and check if it's cooked through. Repeat with the remaining chicken pieces. Serve hot with your favorite red sauce as a dip.

CHICKEN EMPANADAS

Makes 48 pops

1 tablespoon olive oil

2 large boneless, skinless chicken breasts (about 1½ pounds total)

1 teaspoon kosher salt

¼ teaspoon pepper

1 tablespoon ground cumin

3 ounces cream cheese, softened

¼ cup diced red bell peppers

1 (15-ounce) package cold prepared pie dough

8 ounces Colby Jack cheese, cut into 48 pieces

1. Heat the olive oil in a medium skillet over medium-low heat. Season the chicken breasts with the salt, pepper, and cumin, then cook in the pan for about 4 minutes on each side, until cooked through. Let cool, then transfer to a food processor. Pulse about 4 times, until the chicken is shredded, with no large chunks.

2. Transfer the shredded chicken to a medium bowl, then add the cream cheese and diced peppers. Stir to combine.

3. Unroll the pie dough from its packaging and cut into 48 (2-inch) squares. Fill each square with one piece of Colby Jack cheese and then about ¾ tablespoon chicken mixture. Fold opposite ends of the dough together and pinch closed. Shape each one into a round ball.

4. When the cake pop maker is hot, spray with olive oil. Place a dough ball in each well and cook for 3 minutes, until golden brown.

CHICKEN SOUVLAKI BITES

These delicious bites are perfect for a little taste of the Greek life and beat eating out, any day. The herbs give the chicken in this recipe a juicy, savory flavor that everyone will enjoy. *Makes 36 pops*

CHICKEN

3 cloves garlic

2 tablespoons fresh lemon juice

½ small sweet white onion

½ teaspoon crushed red pepper flakes

1 tablespoon Dijon mustard

3 tablespoons olive oil

2 large boneless, skinless chicken breasts (about 1½ pounds total)

1 tablespoon dried oregano

tzatziki, for dipping

salt and pepper

DOUGH

1 (¼-ounce) packet active dry yeast

1 cup warm water

1 teaspoon sugar

2¼ cups all-purpose flour, plus more for dusting

1½ teaspoons olive oil

½ teaspoon salt

1. Prepare the Chicken: In a blender or small food chopper, chop the garlic, lemon juice, onion, red pepper flakes, and mustard. Transfer the mixture to a large zip-top bag. Add the olive oil and chicken. Sprinkle in the oregano and season with salt and pepper. Squeeze or shake the chicken around to evenly coat with all the ingredients. Let marinate overnight or while you make the dough.

2. Prepare the Dough: In a food processor, pulse together the yeast, warm water, and sugar. Remove the blade and let sit for 5 minutes. Then replace the blade and add the flour, olive oil, and salt. Process until the dough clumps into a big ball. Lay out the dough ball on a work surface and shape it into about a 10-inch log. The dough should not be too sticky. If it sticks to the surface, add more flour and work it in. Cover the top of the dough with a piece of plastic wrap and let rest while you cook the chicken.

3. Preheat the oven's broiler and make sure a rack is in the middle of the oven. Line a rimmed baking sheet with aluminum foil, and empty the chicken breasts out into the pan with all the marinade. Broil on high for about 10 minutes, then turn the chicken breasts

over and broil another 10 minutes. The chicken should not be pink on the inside, but not burnt or dry either. Let cool for 5 minutes.

4. Pinch an inch of dough and use a mini rolling pin to roll the piece out to about 3 inches. Then, cut the chicken breasts into 1 x ¾-inch pieces to get about 18 pieces per breast. Place 1 piece of chicken onto each piece of rolled-out dough. Try to get as much of the marinade seasonings to coat the chicken as possible.

5. When the cake pop maker is hot, spray with olive oil. Place 1 dough ball in each well and cook for 3 minutes, until golden brown. Serve with your favorite tzatziki sauce for dipping.

CHICKEN CORDON BLEU

These rarely make it to the table because they get eaten right out of the cake pop maker! This is a much simpler and easier way to cook this fabulous dish without spending the whole day in the kitchen.   *Makes 25 pops*

2 large boneless, skinless chicken breasts (about 1½ pounds total)

4 slices deli ham

4 slices Swiss cheese

40 Ritz crackers

2 large eggs

1 tablespoon whole milk

1. Cut the chicken into 1-inch cubes, for about 25 cubes. Using a knife, make a slit in the center of each chicken cube. Prepare the filling by layering 1 slice of ham and 1 slice of Swiss cheese on a cutting board. Cut them into ½ x 3-inch strips. Next, roll each ham and cheese strip together into a log and insert it into the slit in the raw chicken.

2. In a medium bowl, crush the Ritz crackers into crumbs. In a small bowl, beat the eggs with the milk. Bathe the filled chicken in the eggs and then coat with the cracker crumbs. Continue until all the chicken pieces are coated.

3. When the cake pop maker is hot, spray with olive oil. Place a chicken piece in each of about 8 wells and cook for 4 to 4½ minutes, until the chicken is no longer pink on the inside. Repeat with the remaining chicken pieces.

CHICKEN FLORENTINE ROLLS

Chicken Florentine mixes juicy chicken, spinach, and a cream sauce into a wonderful meal. It's satisfying when you can incorporate veggies into a delicious pop. These are great for a family meal or a special dinner for two paired with a bottle of Pinot Grigio. Molto buono!   *Makes 24 pops*

1 tablespoon olive oil

1 pound chicken cutlets

2 cloves garlic, minced

5 ounces baby spinach

4 ounces grated Gruyère cheese

2 tablespoons grated Pecorino-Romano cheese

1 (10.5-ounce) can cream of chicken soup

2 (7.5-ounce) tubes biscuits

1. Heat the olive oil in a large skillet over medium heat. Add the chicken and garlic and cook for about 3 minutes undisturbed, then turn the chicken and shred it into mini pieces. Add the spinach and cook both together for 4 more minutes, until the chicken is cooked through. Cool and transfer to a large bowl.

2. Add the grated Gruyère and Pecorino-Romano cheeses to the chicken and spinach mixture. Then add the cream of chicken soup and stir to combine.

3. Separate the biscuits and cut each biscuit in half. Use a mini rolling pin to roll out each half biscuit. Add about 1 teaspoon of chicken mixture to each square and pinch opposite ends of the dough together to form a ball.

4. When the cake pop maker is hot, spray with olive oil. Place 1 dough ball in each well and cook for 3 minutes, until golden brown.

CHICKEN MEATBALLS FOR KIDS

These are my favorite guilt-free chicken nuggets and are a staple in my house for busy weeknight dinners. If I have leftover Chinese food, I use ¾ cup vegetable fried rice in place of the rice and vegetables in this recipe.   *Makes 21 pops*

1 pound ground chicken

⅓ cup corn kernels

⅓ cup green peas

¾ cup cooked white rice

1 large egg

½ tablespoon dried minced onion

½ tablespoon kosher salt

¼ cup panko breadcrumbs

¼ cup grated Parmesan cheese

1. Combine all the ingredients in a large bowl. Roll the mixture into meatballs of about 1½ tablespoons each. I use a cookie scoop that holds 1½ tablespoons, which helps to measure the meatballs correctly.

2. When the cake pop maker is hot, spray with olive oil. Fill each of 6 to 8 wells with a meatball and cook for 4 minutes, until brown and cooked through.

VARIATIONS: Instead of peas, try using ⅓ cup grated zucchini.

CHICKEN BURRITO POPS

This recipe also works well with ½ pound of ground beef, ground turkey, or ¾-inch beef chunks. For the black beans and rice, I prefer Zatarain's brand New Orleans Style. *Makes 48 pops*

CHICKEN

2 large boneless, skinless chicken breasts (1½ pounds total) or 1½ pounds boneless skinless thigh meat

8 ounces Monterey Jack cheese, divided into 48 very small pieces

1 (7-ounce) box black beans and rice, prepared according to the package directions

DOUGH

3 cups all-purpose flour

1 teaspoon salt

2 tablespoons taco seasoning

¼ cup vegetable oil

¾ to 1 cup water, as needed

sour cream, salsa, and guacamole, to serve

1. Prepare the Chicken: Set a medium skillet over medium heat and spray the pan with olive oil. Season the chicken with salt and pepper and then cook the chicken on each side for about 4 minutes, until cooked through. Let cool, and cut the chicken into ½-inch cubes. Set aside.

2. Prepare the Dough: In a food processor, combine the flour, salt, taco seasoning, and oil. Then slowly add the water until a dough ball forms. The dough should not be too dry or too wet.

3. Pinch off a 1-inch ball of dough. Roll out the dough piece to about 3 inches in diameter using a mini rolling pin. Top the dough with 1 piece of cheese, 1 cube of chicken, and then ½ tablespoon of rice mixture. Pinch the dough closed over the filling. Repeat with the remaining ingredients.

4. When the cake pop maker is hot, spray with vegetable oil or sunflower oil. Place 1 dough ball in each well and cook for 3½ minutes, until light golden brown. Serve with sour cream, salsa, and guacamole.

TURKEY TEA SANDWICHES

Makes 20 pops

6½ ounces spreadable vegetable or
garlic-herb cream cheese

5 thick slices oven-roasted turkey breast
(from the deli counter)

1 (7.5-ounce) tube home-style biscuits

1. Spread about 3 tablespoons cream cheese spread on each slice of turkey. Then roll each turkey slice into a log. Cut each log into ¾-inch slices.

2. Separate the biscuits and cut each one in half. Use a mini rolling pin to roll out each half. Place one ¾-inch section of turkey roll-up in the center of each biscuit half. Pinch the dough over the turkey filling to close.

3. When the cake pop maker is hot, spray with sunflower or vegetable oil. Place 1 dough ball in each well and cook for 2 minutes, until golden brown. These are best served at room temperature.

TURKEY-BRIE BURGERS WITH GARLIC-HERB MAYO

Makes 20 pops

1 pound lean ground turkey meat

⅓ cup chopped fresh parsley

1 tablespoon garlic powder

1 tablespoon dried minced onion

pinch of pepper, or to taste

5 ounces Brie cheese

salt

1 recipe Savory Bites Bread Dough (page 91)

Garlic-Herb Mayo, for dipping (recipe follows)

1. Preheat the oven to 325°F degrees. In a large bowl, combine the turkey, parsley, garlic powder, onion, and pepper. Roll the mixture into 1-inch balls, for a total of about 20. Make a well in each ball and scoop 1 teaspoon of the Brie into the well. Close the meat around the cheese to form a ball again. Place on a cookie sheet lined with parchment paper. Season the filled balls with salt. Bake for 10 minutes.

2. Divide the dough into 24 (2-inch) squares. Use a mini rolling pin to roll out each dough square so it's 3 to 4 inches and place 1 meatball in the middle each square. Pinch the dough ends together over the meatball to seal it inside.

3. When the cake pop maker is hot, spray with olive oil. Place a dough ball in each well and cook for 1 to 2 minutes, until light golden brown. Serve with garlic-herb mayo.

GARLIC-HERB MAYO

½ cup shredded fresh basil

4 cloves garlic

1 cup regular or light mayonnaise

¼ teaspoon salt

1. In a food processor, pulse the basil and garlic together until minced. In a medium bowl, stir together the mayonnaise and basil-garlic mixture until combined. Season with salt. Serve as a dip for the turkey burgers.

DAY AFTER TURKEY DAY POPS

Makes 24 pops

1½ cups finely diced leftover turkey meat

½ cup turkey gravy

¾ cup shredded mozzarella cheese

1 (8-ounce) tube seamless crescent dough

1. Combine the turkey, gravy, and cheese in a medium bowl.

2. Roll out the crescent dough and divide into 24 (2-inch) squares. Use a mini rolling pin to roll out each square and fill with a heaping ½ teaspoon of the turkey mixture. Fold the dough over the turkey mixture, pinching the seams together.

3. When the cake pop maker is hot, place 1 dough ball in each well and cook for 4 minutes, until medium golden brown.

FISH 'N' CHIPS

I love asking kids, "Who wants potato chips for dinner?" This gets them excited every time. Plus, this recipe is super easy for even them to make. But secretly, I love these bites just as much as they do.   *Makes 24 pops*

1 pound cod fillet (about 1½ inches thick)

3 large eggs

1 (8-ounce) bag potato chips

tartar sauce, ketchup, or malted vinegar, to serve

1. Cut the cod into generous 1½ x 1-inch nuggets. In a medium bowl, beat the eggs. In a food processor, pulse the potato chips to a crumb consistency. Place the crumbs on a large plate. Bathe the fish nuggets in eggs, then coat with the potato chip crumbs.

2. When the cake pop maker is hot, spray lightly with olive oil. Place 1 nugget in each well and cook for 5 to 6 minutes, until golden brown. Serve with tartar sauce, ketchup, or malted vinegar.

HEATHER'S FAMOUS SEAFOOD PAELLA

This recipe is great for intimate family gatherings or an evening with friends. It is a great way to utilize the cake pop maker for embellishing a great meal. It's always a crowd pleaser and is super easy and quick to make once you get accustomed to preparing it. For an elegant presentation, serve in martini glasses, sold at party stores in bulk.   *Serves 6 as an entree, or 12 as a side dish*

2 (27-ounce) cans sea clam juice

2 tablespoons olive oil

1 large sweet white onion, diced

1 large red bell pepper, diced

8 ounces chorizo, casing removed

crushed red pepper flakes

1 (8-ounce) box Spanish-style yellow rice

1 cup dry white wine

1½ pounds large shrimp (31–40 count)

24 mussels, scrubbed and debearded

½ pound bay scallops (optional)

12 small cherry stone clams (optional)

1 recipe Savory Bites Bread Dough (page 91)

1. In a large saucepan, pour the 2 cans of sea juice. Fill 1 empty can with 27 ounces of water and add to the pan. Bring to a boil over high heat. Then reduce the heat to low and let simmer.

2. Warm 2 tablespoons olive oil in a large sauté pan or skillet over medium heat, and add the onion. Cook for 3 minutes, stirring. Then add the bell pepper and cook for 3 more minutes, stirring. Next, add the chorizo, breaking it up with a fork, and cook for about 4 minutes, until cooked. Add the desired amount of red pepper flakes (I use about 1 tablespoon). Add the box of rice to the mixture and cook, stirring, for 2 minutes. Add the white wine and cook for 2 minutes more. Turn off the heat.

3. Transfer the contents of the sauté pan or skillet into the simmering saucepan of sea clam juice. Let continue simmering on low heat for about 15 minutes, until the rice is softened, stirring occasionally. Add the shrimp, mussels, and scallops and clams, if using. Cover and let cook for about 10 minutes until the seafood is cooked through, stirring occasionally.

4. To prepare the bread, cut the dough into 24 (2-inch) squares and roll each one into a ball. When the cake pop maker is hot, place 1 ball in each well and cook for 2 minutes. Serve with the paella.

CLAM BITES

Serve these at a party or dinner in empty clam shells for a fun presentation.

Makes 15 pops

1 cup water

1 dozen little neck clams

1 (6½-ounce) can chopped sea clams

1 cup Italian-style breadcrumbs

2 tablespoons unsalted butter, melted

½ teaspoon kosher salt

4 fresh basil leaves, shredded

1 large egg

2 tablespoons dry white wine

½ teaspoon crushed red pepper flakes

1. In a medium saucepan over medium-high heat, bring the water to a boil, then add the clams. Cover and steam them for about 5 minutes. Pull them out as they open, otherwise they'll overcook. Remove the clam meat from the shells, chop the meat, and place in a medium bowl. Reserve the empty shells.

2. To the clams in the bowl, add the can of clams with their juices along with the breadcrumbs, butter, salt, basil, egg, wine, and red pepper flakes. Stir to combine.

3. When the cake pop maker is hot, spray with olive oil. Scoop the clam mixture by generous tablespoons and then roll into balls using your hands. To be sure the balls are the right size, cook just 1 ball for 4 to 5 minutes, until dark golden brown. Adjust the ball size as needed, then cook the remaining balls in 2 batches. Serve the cooked clam bites in the empty clam shells.

AHI TUNA WRAP WITH LIME-SOUR CREAM DIP

Makes 24 pops

¾ pound ahi tuna steak

8 ounces baby spinach, stems removed

1 tablespoon olive oil

½ medium avocado, diced

½ large tomato, diced

⅓ cup fresh cilantro, shredded

1 cup sour cream

2 tablespoons mayonnaise

1 teaspoon lime zest

2 tablespoons fresh lime juice

1 recipe Savory Bites Tortilla Dough (page 35)

salt and pepper

1. Drizzle the tuna steak with the olive oil and season with salt and pepper. In a small sauté pan or skillet over medium-high heat, sear the tuna steak for 1½ minutes on each side. Cut the cooked tuna into ½-inch squares.

2. Gently combine the avocado, tomato, and cilantro in a small bowl. Season with a pinch of salt. In another small bowl, combine the sour cream, mayonnaise, and lime zest and juice. Stir and season with salt to taste. Refrigerate until ready to serve.

3. Roll out the tortilla dough and cut into 2-inch squares. Use a mini rolling pin to roll out each square so it's 3 to 4 inches. Place 3 spinach leaves, 1 tuna cube, and 1 teaspoon of tomato mixture in the center of each piece of dough. Wrap the dough over the filling and pinch the ends of the dough closed.

4. When the cake pop maker is hot, spray with sunflower or vegetable oil. Place 1 dough ball in each well and cook for 4 minutes, until golden brown. Serve warm, with the lime–sour cream dip.

BEST TUNA MELTS

Makes 12 pops

1 (6-ounce) can solid white tuna in water, drained

2 tablespoons mayonnaise

1 tablespoon minced celery

1 tablespoon minced onion

1 medium, ripe tomato

2 thick slices Swiss cheese

12 squares (½ recipe) Savory Bites Bread Dough (page 91)

salt and pepper

1. In a small bowl, combine the tuna, mayonnaise, celery, and onion, and season with pepper. Remove the seeds from the tomato, and cut into ¾-inch squares. Season with salt. Cut the Swiss cheese into 1-inch squares. Roll out each of the bread dough squares with a mini rolling pin to 3 to 4 inches.

2. On each dough square stack a tomato piece, then a ½ tablespoon scoop of tuna, then top with a cheese square. Pinch opposite ends of the dough over the tuna filling and shape into a ball.

3. When the cake pop maker is hot, spray with sunflower or vegetable oil. Place a dough ball in each well and cook for 3 minutes, until light golden brown.

VARIATIONS: Add a ¾-inch square of cooked bacon on top of the tuna and then top with the Swiss cheese.

LOBSTER MANGO BURRITO POPS

Makes 20 pops

TORTILLA DOUGH

3 cups all-purpose flour

1 teaspoon salt

¼ cup vegetable oil

1 cup water

FILLING

1 large mango, diced

1 (8-ounce) package cooked and peeled langostino lobster tails, defrosted (in the freezer section of the supermarket)

½ red onion, chopped

2 tablespoons chopped fresh cilantro, chopped

1 jalapeño pepper or serrano chile, chopped (optional)

1 tablespoon fresh lime juice

½ teaspoon salt

sour cream, to serve

1. Prepare the Tortilla Dough: Combine all the dough ingredients in a food processor and pulse until ball forms. Cover with plastic wrap to retain moisture.

2. Prepare the Filling: In a large bowl, combine the mango, lobster, onion, cilantro, chile, lime juice, and salt. Mix to combine.

3. Pinch a 1-inch piece of dough and use a mini rolling pin to roll it out to a 3 to 4-inch circle. Fill with 1 tablespoon of the lobster-mango mixture. Pinch the dough sides closed over the filling. Repeat with the remaining ingredients.

4. When the cake pop is hot, spray with sunflower or vegetable oil. Place 1 dough ball in each well and cook for 3 to 4 minutes, until golden. Serve with sour cream.

LOBSTER AND SHRIMP RISOTTO BITES

Makes 40 pops

12 ounces Arborio rice

1 (14.5-ounce) can chicken broth

1 (10.5-ounce) can lobster bisque soup

1/2 cup whole milk

1 cup grated Parmesan cheese

1/2 pound shrimp, boiled or steamed

1/4 pound lobster tail, boiled or steamed

salt and pepper

1. In a microwave-safe bowl or casserole dish, stir together the uncooked rice and the chicken broth. Cover and microwave for 3 minutes on high power. Remove from the microwave, stir the rice, and microwave for another 3 minutes. (Because microwave times may vary, be sure when stirring the rice that it does not become too dry. You can always add some more broth if you need to.) Next, stir in the lobster bisque soup, return to the microwave, and cook for another 3 minutes. Remove from the microwave and stir in the milk and Parmesan cheese. Season with salt and pepper and then cover and let sit until the milk has been absorbed, about 5 minutes.

2. After broiling or steaming the shrimp and lobster, remove any shells or tails still remaining. Next, chop the shrimp into 1/4-inch pieces and shred the lobster meat. When all the liquids are absorbed into the rice, add the seafood.

3. When the cake pop maker is hot, spray with olive oil. Scoop the rice mixture into 1½-tablespoon balls; a 1-tablespoon cookie scoop is the easiest way to measure the perfect size for these pops. Place each ball in a well and cook for 4 minutes, until medium golden brown. Serve warm.

BROCCOLI CHEESE RISOTTO BITES: Omit the lobster bisque soup, shrimp, lobster, and Parmesan cheese. Add a 10.5-ounce can of broccoli cheese soup and 1 cup steamed, chopped broccoli, 1/2 pound diced, cooked chicken, and 1/2 cup shredded cheddar cheese.

SHRIMP SLAW SANDWICHES

Makes 24 pops

2 large eggs

1 tablespoon whole milk

1 cup Italian-style breadcrumbs

3 tablespoons Old Bay seasoning

¼ cup vegetable oil, or as needed, for frying

12 uncooked shrimp (21-24 count), peeled and halved

kosher salt

1 recipe Savory Bites Bread Dough (page 91)

8 ounces prepared coleslaw

1. In a small bowl, beat together the eggs and milk. In a medium bowl, combine the breadcrumbs and Old Bay seasoning. Pour about ¼ cup of vegetable oil in a medium frying pan or heavy skillet over medium heat. Heat to about 230°F. Bathe each half shrimp in the egg wash, then dip each piece in the breadcrumbs. Cook the coated shrimp in the hot oil on both sides until a medium golden brown, about 4 minutes total. Remove the shrimp from the pan and let cool on a paper towel. When cool, sprinkle with salt.

2. Cut the bread dough into 24 (2-inch) squares. Use a mini rolling pin to roll out each square so it's 3 to 4 inches. Then place 1 teaspoon of coleslaw and a 1-inch segment of fried shrimp on each rolled-out dough piece. Pinch the ends of the dough together over the shrimp filling to close.

3. When the cake pop maker is hot, spray with sunflower or vegetable oil. Place a dough ball in each well and cook for 1 to 2 minutes, until medium golden brown. These can be made ahead of time and taste best when served at room temperature.

SALMON AND SPINACH ALFREDO BITES

You can easily replace the salmon in this recipe with boneless, skinless chicken breast. *Makes 30 pops*

SALMON

1 small white sweet onion

1 tablespoon extra-virgin olive oil

2 cloves garlic

4 fresh basil leaves

1¼ pounds salmon fillet

salt and pepper

DOUGH

2 cups all-purpose flour

½ teaspoon baking powder

½ teaspoon salt

3 large eggs

2 tablespoons extra-virgin olive oil

1 tablespoon water

SAUCE

1 large shallot, finely minced

2 cloves garlic, finely minced

1 tablespoon extra-virgin olive oil

2 tablespoons butter

2 tablespoons all-purpose flour

2 cups light cream

1 cup grated Parmesan cheese

1 (9-ounce) bag spinach, steamed and shredded

salt and pepper

1. Prepare the Salmon: Preheat the oven's broiler to high and place a rack in the center of the oven. In a mini chopper, process the onion, oil, garlic, and basil leaves. Alternatively, you can finely mince these ingredients. This will leave you with a thick mashed purée. Spread this purée on the salmon fillet and sprinkle with salt and freshly ground pepper. Broil for 20 minutes. Then take the salmon out and check to see if it is fully cooked; it's done when you can easily separate it into flakes with a fork. If not, cover with aluminum foil to prevent burning and cook another 5 minutes. After thoroughly cooked, remove from the oven and allow to cool. While the salmon is broiling, begin making the dough.

2. Prepare the Dough: If you have a stand mixer, fit it with the dough hook. If not, use a large bowl and your hands to work the dough. Combine the flour, baking powder, salt, eggs, olive oil, and water until a ball forms. The dough should not be too sticky or dry. Adjust the consistency with either ½ tablespoon of water or sprinkle with more flour. Knead the dough on the counter for 2

minutes, then cover with a piece of plastic wrap and let it rest for 30 minutes.

3. Prepare the Sauce: Finely chop the shallot and garlic. In a large sauté pan or skillet, heat the oil and butter over medium heat. Add the shallot and garlic, cook for 2 minutes, stirring, and then add the flour. Stir with a whisk for about 2 minutes more and then add the cream. Continue cooking and stirring for 4 minutes; the sauce will begin to thicken. Remove from the heat and stir in the Parmesan cheese and spinach. Allow to cool.

4. Slice the salmon into 1 x ¾-inch segments. When the cake pop maker is hot, spray with olive oil. Then, pinch an inch of dough and use a mini rolling pin to roll out the dough piece so it's 3 to 4 inches and about ⅛ inch thick. Scoop ½ tablespoon of the spinach mixture into the center of each dough piece and top with 1 salmon segment. Pinch the ends of the dough together over the filling to close. Place 1 dough ball in each well and cook for 3 minutes, until golden brown. To prevent the filling from leaking out, place filled dough balls with the seams facing up. Serve warm.

BEEF, PORK, AND LAMB

BACON-BLUE BURGERS

Makes 30 pops

4 slices thinly sliced bacon, cooked until crisp and crushed into bits

2 cloves garlic, minced

1 pound lean ground beef (90% lean)

2 ounces cream cheese

¼ cup crumbled blue cheese

2 (7.5-ounce) tubes home-style biscuits

salt and pepper

1. Preheat the oven to 325°F. Line a cookie sheet with parchment paper.

2. In a large bowl, add the bacon and garlic to the ground beef. Season with freshly ground pepper and then thoroughly mix the ingredients with your hands or a fork. In a small bowl, add the cream cheese to the blue cheese. Combine well with a fork, and set aside.

3. Scoop out 30 equal size balls of meat, each about 1 inch in diameter. Poke each ball with a finger and fill it with a ½ teaspoon scoop of the cheese mixture. Close the meat over the cheese, so the cheese is in the middle of the meat. Roll into a perfect ball with your hands and place on the parchment-lined cookie sheet. Season with salt. Bake for 10 minutes; be sure not to overcook. Allow to cool slightly.

4. Separate the biscuits and slice each one in half. Roll out each biscuit half with a mini rolling pin, and place 1 meatball on each biscuit. Pinch the dough over the meatballs to close. When the cake pop maker is hot, place 1 dough ball in each well and cook for 1½ minutes, until lightly golden.

CHEESEBURGER POPS FOR KIDS

Makes 20 pops

1 pound ground beef (90% lean)

2 tablespoons minced onions

1 (7.5-ounce) tube home-style biscuits

5 slices American cheese, quartered

ketchup, to serve

1. Preheat the oven to 350°F and spray a medium baking sheet with olive oil. In a large bowl, combine the ground beef and minced onions with your hands or a fork. Roll the mixture into 1¼-inch balls and place on the prepared sheet. Bake for 10 minutes and then let cool completely.

2. Separate the biscuits and cut each one in half. Stretch the dough with your thumbs and add a quarter of a slice of cheese and 1 meatball inside. Stretch the dough over mixture and pinch closed.

3. When the cake pop maker is hot, spray with olive oil. Place 1 ball in each well and cook for 3 minutes, until golden brown. Serve with ketchup.

BACON-CHEDDAR BURGERS

Makes 30 pops

3/4 pound ground beef (90% lean)

2 tablespoons finely chopped sweet onions

4 ounces mild cheddar cheese

4 slices uncooked bacon

1 recipe Savory Bites Bread Dough (page 91)

salt and pepper

1. Preheat the oven to 325°F and line a cookie sheet with parchment paper. In a large bowl, combine the ground beef and onions. Season with freshly ground pepper and combine ingredients with a fork.

2. Cut the cheddar cheese into 1 x ½-inch pieces. Roll the meat into 15 (1-inch) balls. Poke the meat with a finger and insert 1 cheese piece into each meatball. Wrap the meat around the cheese to form a ball again. Now, cut the bacon into 4-inch strips and wrap 1 strip around each meatball. Place on the parchment-lined cookie sheet and season with salt. Bake for 10 minutes; be sure not to overcook.

3. Roll out each dough square with a mini rolling pin. When the meatballs come out of the oven, allow to cool for 3 minutes, then use a sharp knife to cut each one right down the middle. Then place one half meatball on each rolled-out dough square, and close the dough over the meat. When the cake pop maker is hot, place a dough ball in each well and cook for 2 minutes, until golden brown.

CHILI CHEESE DOGS

Use your favorite chili for these dogs. I like Hormel Chili with No Beans.

Makes 24 pops

5 long hot dogs (longer than standard bun size)

1 (4-ounce block) Velveeta cheese

1 recipe Savory Bites Bread Dough (page 91)

1 (15-ounce can) chili

1. Cut a slit down the entire length of each hot dog and place on a microwave-safe plate. Microwave for about 1 minute on high power until the hot dogs open up. Cut the hot dogs into 1¼-inch lengths. One hot dog should be able to be divided into 5 pieces. Cut the Velveeta into ¼-inch slices that are 1 inch long and ½ inch wide.

2. Divide the bread dough into 24 (2-inch) squares. Use a mini rolling pin to roll out each square so it's 3 to 4 inches. Place 1 hot dog section on each rolled-out square, then scoop ½ teaspoon chili into the slit in the hot dog. Top with a piece of Velveeta. Pinch opposite ends of the dough together to form a ball.

3. When the cake pop maker is hot, spray with olive oil. Cook the dough balls for 3 minutes, until golden brown.

VARIATIONS: Instead of chili and cheese filling, you can scoop ½ teaspoon of sauerkraut on the hot dogs. Serve with yellow mustard.

FRENCH ONION SOUP

Makes 24 pops

2 tablespoons sweet cream butter

2 small sweet white onions, chopped

1 clove garlic, minced

¼ cup dry red wine

1 (14.5-ounce) can beef broth

salt and pepper

2 slices white sandwich bread

6 thin slices Swiss cheese

1 (8-ounce) tube seamless crescent dough

1. In a medium saucepan over medium heat, melt the butter. Add the onions and garlic. Season with salt and pepper, and cook for about 6 minutes. Add the red wine and cook about 4 more minutes. Add the beef broth and let simmer for 5 minutes. Remove from the heat and let cool.

2. Preheat a toaster oven or the standard oven's broiler to high. Cut the bread into 1-inch squares. I got about 12 squares from each slice. Put the squares on a piece of aluminum foil and then add 3 thin slices of cheese on top of each bread square. Toast the cheese bread in the oven for about 5 minutes or until cheese has completely melted, then separate squares. On a large plate, pour in about ½ cup onion broth. Place the toasted cheese bread squares into the broth on the plate and let soak for about 4 minutes.

3. Roll out the crescent dough and divide into 24 (2-inch) squares. Use a mini rolling pin to roll out each square. Fill each dough square with 1 teaspoon onions, then top it with one square of cheesy bread. Pinch opposite ends of the dough together to form a ball. When the cake pop maker is hot, place 1 dough ball in each well and cook for 3 to 4 minutes, until golden brown.

PHILLY CHEESE STEAK POPS

Makes 24 pops

1 tablespoon extra-virgin olive oil

½ large green bell pepper, diced

½ medium sweet white onion, diced

¼ pound provolone cheese, thinly sliced

¼ pound rare roast beef, thinly sliced (about 8 slices)

1 recipe Savory Bites Bread Dough (page 91)

ketchup, to serve

1. Heat the olive oil in a large sauté pan or skillet over medium heat. Add the pepper and onion, and sauté for 5 minutes, then let cool.

2. Layer 4 slices of the provolone cheese about 6 inches in width. Stack 4 slices of roast beef on top of the cheese. Cut the stack into 6 equal 1-inch sections, then in half. In total you should have 12 (1-inch) squares. Repeat with the remaining roast beef and cheese.

3. Spread out the bread dough and divide it into 24 (2-inch) squares. Roll out each square with a mini rolling pin. Scoop about ½ teaspoon of peppers and onions onto each dough square, and top with a square of roast beef and cheese. Wrap opposite corners of dough together over the mixture to form a ball.

4. When the cake pop maker is hot, spray with olive oil. Place a dough ball in each well and cook for 4 minutes, until golden brown. Serve with ketchup.

BEEF WELLINGTON BITES

These are great for parties. They have an exquisite flavor without you spending the whole day in the kitchen preparing them. You'll definitely stun your guests!

Makes 16 pops

1 (10-ounce) container cremini mushrooms

1 large shallot

1 clove garlic

1 tablespoon sweet cream butter

1½ pounds beef fillet, cut into 1-inch cubes

½ tablespoon olive oil

1 (8-ounce) tube seamless crescent dough

salt and pepper

1. Place the mushrooms, shallot, and garlic in a food processor and pulse until well blended, about 2 minutes. In a large sauté pan or skillet over medium heat, melt the butter. Add the mushroom mixture and sauté for about 8 minutes to reduce the liquid. Season with salt and pepper. Set aside.

2. Coat the beef cubes with olive oil and season with salt and pepper. Heat a large skillet over medium heat, and sear the meat cubes. Toss until brown all over, under 2 minutes. Be careful not to let the beef cook through! Let cool while preparing the dough.

3. Roll out the crescent dough and divide into 16 (3-inch) squares. Fill each square with ¼ teaspoon of mushroom paste and top with 1 beef cube. Pinch the opposite ends of the dough together to seal. When the cake pop maker is hot, place a dough ball in each well and cook 2 minutes, until golden brown.

SHEPHERD'S PIE

This is probably one of the most difficult recipes in this book to make, but it's also one of the tastiest! The key is to make sure the proportion of potato to meat filling is correct.   *Makes 25 pops*

POTATOES

1 pound mini red potatoes

1 small carrot

¼ cup (½ stick) sweet cream butter

2 cloves garlic, minced

⅓ cup light cream

¼ cup all-purpose flour

1 large egg yolk

¼ cup grated Parmesan cheese

salt and pepper

MEAT FILLING

½ tablespoon olive oil

½ cup diced sweet white onion

3 cloves garlic, minced

½ pound ground beef (85% lean)

1 tablespoon all-purpose flour

½ teaspoon Worcestershire sauce

¼ cup beef broth

¼ cup corn kernels

1 tablespoon shredded fresh parsley

salt and pepper

1. Prepare the Potatoes: Place the potatoes and carrot in a medium saucepan filled halfway with cold water. Cook over high heat until it begins to boil. Then turn down the heat to a simmer. Cook about 10 minutes until the potatoes are soft, or you can easily poke a fork through them.

2. While the potatoes are simmering, melt the butter in a small sauté pan or skillet over medium heat. When the butter is melted, add the 2 cloves minced garlic. Cook for 2 minutes and then add the light cream. Season with salt and pepper. Stir to prevent it from scalding. Cook the cream mixture on a light simmer for 2 more minutes, then remove from the heat.

3. Once the potatoes are soft, drain the liquid. Dice the carrot and reserve for later in recipe. Transfer the cooked potatoes to a large bowl or a stand mixer fitted with the paddle attachment. Mash the potatoes and add the cream mixture until the potatoes are smooth. Let sit to cool. When cool, add the flour, egg yolk, and Parmesan cheese. Stir to combine and season with salt, as needed.

4. Prepare the Meat Filling: In a large skillet, over medium heat, warm the olive oil. Then, add the diced onion and minced garlic. Cook for about 2 minutes, until the onions are soft and then add the ground beef. Cook until the beef is browned and cooked through, about 4 minutes. Line a plate with a paper towel and transfer the cooked beef to the plate to drain any excess grease. Then return the beef to the skillet over medium heat. Sprinkle the flour over the meat and add the Worcestershire sauce, beef broth, corn, diced carrot, and fresh parsley. Combine all ingredients well and season with salt and pepper. Remove from the heat and let cool.

5. Scoop an even tablespoon of potato mixture into the palm of your hand. Squish the potato with your three middle fingers to make a flat surface. Scoop an even ½ tablespoon of meat mixture into the center of the flattened potato. Gently wrap potato over the meat filling. This will not be a perfect pocket, but it will still work. (Most important is that the proportions are correct.) Repeat with the remaining ingredients.

6. When the cake pop maker is hot, spray with olive oil. Fill 8 to 10 of the wells with the potato-meatballs. Cook for 4 minutes, until golden. For the most part, these pop right out; however, if the pop is mushy, it could mean you didn't use enough potato mixture. If the balls separate when you try to pop them out, you've used too much of the potato mixture. Don't forget to try cooking 1 pop as a tester before filling the machine. The key is to make sure they are the right size. Your best bet is to use a small spoon to scoop out difficult ones.

FLANK STEAK FAJITAS

Makes 60 pops

STEAK

1 pound flank steak

¼ cup olive oil

¼ cup balsamic vinegar

juice of ½ lemon

1 tablespoon Worcestershire sauce

1 tablespoon Dijon mustard

2 cloves garlic, minced

1 small sweet white onion

TOPPINGS

1 tablespoon olive oil

1 large green bell pepper, diced

1 large red bell pepper, diced

1 jalapeño pepper, diced

1 large sweet white onion, chopped

salt and pepper

DOUGH

3 cups all-purpose flour

1 teaspoon salt

¼ cup vegetable oil

2 tablespoons taco seasoning

1 cup water

1. Prepare the Steak: Season the steak with salt and pepper and then place in a large zip-top bag. Add the other marinade ingredients. Refrigerate overnight to marinate.

2. Prepare the Toppings: In a large sauté pan or skillet over medium heat, warm the olive oil. Add the peppers and onion, and sauté until soft, about 10 minutes. Season with salt and pepper and remove from the heat. Keep the peppers in pan with the lid closed until needed.

3. Prepare the Dough: Combine all the ingredients in a food processer. Pulse until a dough ball forms, then lay it out on the counter with plastic wrap on top to prevent it from drying out. The dough should be soft and slightly sticky, but not sticking to your hands.

4. Fire up the grill on medium-high. Grill the steak for about 4 minutes per side. The inside should be medium-well done, about 160°F when checked with a meat thermometer. Remove from the grill and let cool.

5. Get ready to assemble the fajitas. Be sure the peppers and onions are chopped small enough. Then cut the meat into thin slices, and cut each slice into 1½-inch sections.

6. When the cake pop maker is hot, spray with sunflower or vegetable oil. Next, pinch an inch size of dough and roll it out using a mini rolling pin so it's 3 to 4 inches. Place a slice of meat on the dough, then scoop ½ tablespoon of peppers and onions onto the meat. Pinch the ends of the dough together over the filling. Repeat with the remaining ingredients. Place a dough ball in each well and cook for 3½ minutes, until golden brown. Serve warm.

BEEF TENDERLOIN AND SPINACH WITH BRANDY-CREAM SAUCE

To serve these at a party, skewer two at a time onto a wooden coffee stir stick and serve them along with the cream sauce in a shot glass. This allows for better portion control and helps prevent double dipping. *Makes 24 pops*

6 ounces baby spinach

2 tablespoons olive oil, divided

1 clove garlic, minced

¾ pound beef tenderloin (no more than 2 inches thick)

2 tablespoons sweet cream butter

1 large shallot, minced

¼ cup brandy

½ cup beef broth

½ cup heavy cream

1 (8-ounce) tube seamless crescent dough

salt and pepper

1. To steam the spinach, warm 1 tablespoon of the olive oil and the garlic in a medium saucepan over medium heat. Let cook for 1 minute, then add the spinach leaves. Cook for 2 minutes with the lid on, and then remove from the stove. Do not remove the lid until needed, so it can continue to steam.

2. To prepare the beef tenderloin, preheat the oven's broiler on high. Season the beef by drizzling with the remaining 1 tablespoon olive oil and seasoning with salt and pepper. Broil the steak on high for about 10 minutes. The internal temperature should read between 140 and 145°F (medium-rare) when checked with a meat thermometer. Don't worry if the meat is too pink for you; it will be cooked briefly again in the cake pop maker. Let sit for 5 minutes when it comes out, so it will retain its juices. Meanwhile, shred the spinach, which is now finished steaming. In a medium bowl lined with a paper towel, transfer the shredded spinach to drain any excess liquid.

3. To prepare the brandy cream sauce, melt the butter in a medium sauté pan over medium-high heat. Add the minced shallot and cook for 2 minutes. Stir in the brandy and beef broth and cook for 6 more minutes. The liquid will be reduced by at least half and turn a caramel-brown color. Stir in the heavy cream and season with salt and pepper. Set aside until ready to serve. Cut the cooked beef tenderloin into 1-inch squares. I got 24 pieces from a ¾ pound steak.

4. Roll out the crescent dough and divide into 24 (2-inch) squares. Use a mini rolling pin to roll out the squares to 3 to 4 inches, about ⅛ inch thick. Spoon ½ tablespoon of spinach on to each square and top with one beef cube. Pinch the ends of the dough over the filling to close. When the cake pop maker is hot, place a dough ball in each well and cook for 2½ to 3 minutes until medium-brown in color. Serve with the brandy cream sauce as a dip.

TACO POPPERS

Makes 35 pops

1½ cups all-purpose flour

1 cup cornmeal

1 teaspoon salt

1 teaspoon baking powder

1 cup warm water

¾ pound ground beef (85% lean)

1 small sweet white onion, diced

1 (1-ounce) packet taco seasoning packet

1 medium tomato

½ cup canned black beans, drained

1 cup shredded cheddar cheese

sour cream, for dipping

1. In a food processor, combine the flour, cornmeal, salt, baking powder, and warm water. Pulse until a dough ball forms. Shape the dough ball into a log and cover the top with plastic wrap. Set aside.

2. In a large skillet, brown the beef and onion over medium heat. Sprinkle the taco seasoning packet over the beef while it cooks, and cook until the meat is no longer pink. Transfer to a medium bowl to cool for 2 minutes. While the meat is cooling, dice the tomato, removing the seeds. Then add the tomato, black beans, and cheddar cheese to the beef mixture and stir to combine all the ingredients together.

3. Pinch an inch of dough from the log and roll out using a mini rolling pin. The dough should be rolled as thin as you can without making a hole in it. Fill each piece of dough form with 1 tablespoon of the meat mixture. I prepare 8 meat-filled dough balls at a time, then when the cake pop maker is hot, I place a dough ball in each well and cook them for 4 minutes, until light brown. While those 8 are cooking, I prepare the next batch. Use a dry paper towel to wipe grease off the top plate of the cake pop maker between batches. Serve with sour cream.

VARIATIONS: Add ⅓ cup chopped black olives or 2 tablespoons of chopped green chiles to give it a zestier flavor.

PASTITSIO POPS

This recipe is a Greek delight, but it originates from an Italian dish. It will appeal to a wide range of palates. This is a lovely comfort food, without the guilty feeling. You can eat a couple bite-size morsels and be satisfied. If you do not wish to use ground lamb, beef is an acceptable substitute.   *Makes 30 pops*

DOUGH

2 cups all-purpose flour

½ teaspoon baking powder

½ teaspoon salt

3 large eggs

2 tablespoons extra -virgin olive oil

1 tablespoon water

LAMB MIXTURE

1 pound ground lamb

1 medium sweet white onion, chopped

¾ cup tomato sauce

⅓ cup dry white wine

1 teaspoon ground cinnamon

2 teaspoons salt, divided

3 tablespoons unsalted butter

2 tablespoons all-purpose flour

2 cups whole milk

3 large egg yolks

½ cup grated Parmesan cheese

½ teaspoon ground nutmeg

1. Prepare the Dough: Fit a stand mixer with the dough hook. If you don't have a stand mixer, you can use your hands to work the dough. Combine the flour, baking powder, salt, eggs, olive oil, and water on low speed, or by hand with a spoon, until a dough ball forms. The dough should not be too sticky or too dry. Adjust by adding either ½ tablespoon of water or sprinkling with more flour. Knead the dough on the counter for 2 minutes, then cover with a piece of plastic wrap and allow to rest.

2. Prepare the Lamb Mixture: In a large sauté pan or skillet over medium heat, brown the lamb with the chopped onion. When the meat is no longer pink, carefully drain any excess oil from the pan. Then return to the heat and add the tomato sauce, wine, cinnamon, and 1 teaspoon of the salt. Let simmer until the liquid is reduced at least half, about 12 minutes. Then remove from the heat and let cool.

3. In another large sauté pan or skillet over medium heat, melt the butter. Whisk in the flour and stir for about 2 minutes. Next,

stream in the milk while whisking. Allow the mixture to simmer for 5 minutes, then reduce the heat to low and add the egg yolks one at a time, whisking continually. Simmer the mixture until thickened and creamy. Remove from the heat and stir in the Parmesan cheese, nutmeg, and the remaining 1 teaspoon salt.

4. When the cake pop maker is hot, spray with olive oil. To assemble each pop, pinch an inch of dough and roll out with a mini rolling pin so it's 3 to 4 inches. Scoop 1½ tablespoons of meat mixture and 1 teaspoon of cheese sauce onto the center of the rolled-out dough. Pinch the ends of the dough closed and place a dough ball in each well of the cake pop maker with the seams facing up. Cook for 2 minutes, until golden brown. The perfect-size pop will not be difficult to pinch closed and will have no crust around the middle when finished cooking. Adjust portions if these problems come up.

MONTE CRISTO BITES

Makes 15 pops

4 large eggs

1/3 cup whole milk

1 tablespoon minced onions

6-inch section French bread, cubed

1/3 cup diced ham

1/3 cup diced turkey

1/2 cup shredded Swiss cheese

1. In a medium bowl, whisk the eggs together with the milk. Add the minced onions and bread cubes. Let sit for a few minutes for the bread to soak up the egg mixture. Then break up the soggy bread with a fork.

2. Add the ham, turkey, and Swiss cheese to the egg mixture. Mix all together.

3. When the cake pop maker is hot, spray with sunflower or vegetable oil. Fill each well with 1 tablespoon of batter. Cook for 4 minutes, until golden brown.

PIZZAGAINA POPS (ITALIAN EASTER HAM PIE)

Makes 24 pops

1 slice cooked ham, ¼ inch thick

1 slice provolone cheese, ¼ inch thick

1 slice Parma prosciutto, sliced ¼ inch thick

1 slice pepperoni, ¼ inch thick

1 large hard-boiled egg

2 large uncooked eggs

1½ cups ricotta cheese

1 cup shredded mozzarella cheese

1½ tablespoons grated Parmesan cheese

1 (13-ounce) tube classic pizza dough or other prepared pizza dough

1. Dice the ham, provolone, prosciutto, pepperoni, and hard-boiled egg into ¼-inch cubes. In a large bowl, combine the uncooked eggs with the ricotta, mozzarella, and Parmesan cheeses. Add the diced ingredients to the cheese mixture.

2. Divide the pizza dough into 24 (2-inch) squares. Roll out each square using a mini rolling pin so it's 3 to 4 inches. Scoop a generous ½ tablespoon of egg and meat mixture onto each dough square. Pinch the ends of the dough together and form into balls.

3. When the cake pop maker is hot, spray with olive oil. Place a dough ball in each well and cook for 3 minutes, until golden brown. Serve at room temperature.

THE CUBAN

Makes 24 pops

½ (5-inch) pickle

3 slices boiled ham (about ⅛ pound)

12 slices pork roast (about ½ pound)

6 thin slices Swiss cheese (about ¼ pound)

1 recipe Savory Bites Bread Dough (page 91)

⅓ cup prepared yellow mustard

⅓ cup mayonnaise

1. Cut the pickle lengthwise into 3 long spears. Next, assemble the deli meat as follows to create a pinwheel: First layer 1 slice of ham, then top with pork roast slices. (It will take about 4 pork roast slices to completely cover 1 ham slice). Then layer 2 thin slices of Swiss cheese on top of the pork. Place 1 pickle spear, at the bottom of the meat and cheese layers, and roll into a log. The pickle will then be the center of the log. Repeat until you have 3 meat, cheese, and pickle rolls.

2. Cut the rolls about every ½ inch. This will give you 8 pinwheels for each roll. Divide the bread dough into 24 (2-inch) squares and roll out each square with a mini rolling pin so it's 3 to 4 inches. Place one pinwheel segment in the center of each dough square. Wrap the ends of the dough over the pinwheel and pinch closed.

3. When the cake pop maker is hot, spray with sunflower or vegetable oil. Place a dough ball in each well and cook for 2 to 3 minutes, until light golden brown. In a small bowl, stir together the mustard and mayonnaise. Serve alongside the warm pops as a dip.

JALAPEÑO POPPERS

Makes 24 pops

5 jalapeño peppers (each about 2½ inches long)

4 ounces cream cheese

¼ cup crumbled cooked sausage

¼ cup shredded cheddar cheese

1 (8-ounce) tube seamless crescent dough

1. Cut off the tops of the jalapeños and slice the peppers down the middle lengthwise. Scoop out the seeds and ribs and discard. Place the peppers in a microwave-safe bowl and microwave on high power for 45 seconds. Let cool.

2. In a medium bowl, stir together the cream cheese, sausage, and cheddar cheese. Spoon the cream cheese mixture into the pepper halves; be generous. Then slice the filled peppers into ¾-inch pieces.

3. Roll out the crescent dough and divide into 24 (2-inch) squares. Place 1 cheese-filled pepper piece on each crescent square and pinch opposite ends together to form a ball.

4. When the cake pop maker is hot, place 1 dough ball in each well. Cook for 3½ minutes, until golden brown. Let cool a few minutes before serving; the insides will be extremely hot.

PIZZA POPS

There are many variations of pizza pops, but these are some of my favorites. Depending on how much time I have, I love to make fresh pizza dough. Store-bought is just as tasty, though. *Makes 20 pops*

BASIC PIZZA

1 (13-ounce) tube classic pizza dough or other prepared pizza dough

8 ounces mozzarella cheese, cut into 1-inch cubes

marinara sauce, for dipping

1. Start with room temperature dough. Roll out the dough on a lightly floured surface until about ⅛ inch thick. With a pizza cutter, cut out about 20 (2-inch) squares.

2. Place a cube of mozzarella cheese on each dough square and pinch the opposite ends of the dough together to form a ball.

3. When the cake pop maker is hot, spray with olive oil. Place 1 dough ball in each well and cook for 4 minutes, until golden brown. Serve with your favorite marinara sauce.

SWEET SAUSAGE AND RED PEPPERS: In a large pan, warm 1 tablespoon olive oil over medium-high heat. Cook 4 sausage links, covered, for about 10 minutes, until browned and cooked through. Add 2 diced red bell peppers and sauté for 4 minutes longer. Let the mixture cool. Slice the sausage links to ¼-inch slices. Follow the recipe for Basic Pizza, but add 1 sausage piece on top of the mozzarella cheese in Step 2. Then top with ½ teaspoon of red peppers before moving on to Step 3.

MARGHERITA PIZZA: Follow the recipe for Basic Pizza, but replace the regular mozzarella in Step 2 with fresh 1-inch mozzarella balls that have been marinated in fresh basil and garlic. These are sold in the deli section.

BBQ CHICKEN AND CORN: Set a medium pan over medium heat and spray with olive oil. Coat 2 chicken cutlets with barbecue sauce and lay them in the pan. Cook for about 8 minutes until cooked through, turning once. Add a 4-ounce can of corn to the pan mixture to warm the corn. Dice the chicken into small pieces and let cool to room temperature. Follow the recipe for Basic Pizza, but add 1 teaspoon of chicken and corn mixture to the mozzarella cheese in Step 2.

SPINACH AND FETA: Instead of Step 2, in a large sauté pan or skillet over medium heat, warm 1 tablespoon olive oil, then add 1 teaspoon chopped garlic. Then add 3 cups of baby spinach leaves. Sauté for 3 minutes, and let cool. When the spinach is room temperature, drain any excess liquid and then add 4 ounces crumbled feta cheese and stir to combine. Follow the directions for Basic Pizza, but omit the cheese in Step 2 and instead spoon 1 tablespoon of the spinach mixture onto each dough square and pinch the sides together to close. Then move on to Step 3.

PESTO-PEPPERONI: Follow the recipe for Basic Pizza, but in step 2 add 1 teaspoon prepared pesto and 1-inch wedge of pepperoni sliced ¼-inch thick.

CALZONES FOR KIDS

Makes 24 pops

1 cup ricotta cheese

1½ cups shredded mozzarella cheese

2 tablespoons grated Pecorino-Romano cheese

1 large egg

3 slices thick-cut deli ham

1 (13.8-ounce) tube pizza dough

2 cups marinara or other red sauce, for dipping

salt and pepper

1. In a large bowl, stir together the ricotta, mozzarella, and Pecorino-Romano cheeses and the egg. Season with salt and pepper. Cut the ham slices into 1½-inch squares

2. Roll out the pizza dough and divide into 24 (2-inch) squares. Use a mini rolling pin to roll out each square. Scoop ½ tablespoon of the cheese mixture and 1 cube of ham onto the center of each dough square. Pinch the ends of the dough together over the cheese mixture to close.

3. When the cake pop maker is hot, place 1 dough ball in each well and cook for 3 minutes. When you take these out they will be really hot. Wait 5 minutes before eating. Serve with your favorite marinara sauce for dipping.

PEPPERONI-SAUSAGE STROMBOLI

Stromboli is a mixture of Italian meats and cheeses, but actually is thought to have originated in the United States in the 1950s. To get pepperoni cut to the perfect thickness, have it sliced at your grocer's deli counter. *Makes 48 pops*

¼ pound pepperoni (cut ¼ inch thick)

5 thin slices provolone cheese

3 sausage links (sweet or hot), cooked

1 cup shredded mozzarella cheese

2 tablespoons grated Parmesan cheese

1 teaspoon Italian seasoning

1 recipe Savory Bites Bread Dough (page 91)

2 cups marinara sauce, warmed, for dipping

1. Dice the pepperoni, provolone cheese, and sausage into small pieces. Combine in a medium bowl. Add the shredded mozzarella cheese, grated Parmesan cheese, and Italian seasoning. Stir to combine.

2. Roll out the dough into 24 (2-inch) squares. Using your mini rolling pin, roll out each dough square so it's 3 to 4 inches and fill with 1 tablespoon of the meat and cheese mixture. Close the ends of the dough over the filling and pinch closed.

3. When the cake pop maker is hot, spray the wells with olive oil. Place 1 dough ball in each well and cook for 3 minutes, until golden brown. Let cool for 5 minutes and serve with warm marinara sauce to dip the pops in.

NOT-SO-SLOPPY POPPERS

This recipe calls for beef with a very low fat content. If you use ground beef with a different percentage of fat, just be sure to drain any excess oil from the pan after browning the meat.   *Makes 48 pops*

1 tablespoon olive oil

1 small sweet white onion

2 cloves garlic, minced

1½ pounds extra-lean ground beef (93% lean)

¼ cup diced green peppers

½ cup water

1 (12-ounce) can tomato paste

1 tablespoon prepared deli-style mustard

1 tablespoon Worcestershire sauce

½ teaspoon salt

2 cups shredded mild cheddar cheese

1 recipe Savory Bites Bread Dough (page 91)

1. In a large skillet over medium heat, warm the olive oil, then add the white onion and garlic. Sauté until soft, about 2 minutes, and then add the ground beef. Continue to cook, stirring to evenly brown the meat, for about 8 minutes. Then, add the green peppers, water, and tomato paste. Continue cooking about 5 more minutes, adding the mustard, Worcestershire sauce, and salt while stirring. Stir in the cheese and remove from the heat. Season to taste with additional salt as needed and let cool.

2. Roll out the dough and cut into 48 (1-inch) squares Using your mini rolling pin, roll out the dough squares. Fill each square with 1 tablespoon of beef mixture. Pinch the ends the of the dough closed over the mixture.

3. When the cake pop maker is hot, spray with sunflower or vegetable oil. Place a dough ball in each well and cook for 2 to 2½ minutes, until golden brown. Serve hot.

GRILLED CHEESE WITH BACON

Makes 24 pops

8 ounces creamy Havarti cheese

1 medium plum tomato

6 slices cooked bacon

1 recipe Savory Bites Bread Dough
(page 91)

1. Cut the block of Havarti into 32 equal pieces by dividing it into ½-inch slices. Then separate the ½-inch segments into 3 parts. Next, slice the tomato into ¼-inch-thick slices, then divide each slice into 4 parts. Divide each slice of bacon into ¾-inch squares. Divide the dough into 24 (2-inch) squares and roll out each square with a mini rolling pin so it's 3 to 4 inches.

2. Place a ¾-inch square of bacon, 1 tomato piece, and 1 cheese segment onto the rolled-out dough square. Wrap the dough over the filling and pinch the top closed.

3. When the cake pop maker is hot, spray with sunflower or vegetable oil. Place 1 dough ball in each well and cook for 3 minutes, until golden brown. Let cool for 5 minutes before serving.

PULLED PORK PARTY BITES

These are great to eat while watching football on Sundays, or at any other function where you need to feed a big crowd easily. You'll find packaged pulled pork in the refrigerated meat case section of your grocery store. I like the Jack Daniel's Brand.   *Makes 40 pops*

2 (8.5-ounce) boxes Jiffy Corn Muffin Mix

16 ounces seasoned and cooked pulled pork with barbecue sauce

1. In a large bowl, prepare the corn muffin batter according to the directions. Drain as much sauce and juice from the pulled pork as possible. Add the pulled pork to the batter and stir to combine.

2. When the cake pop maker is hot, spray with sunflower or vegetable oil. Fill each well with 1 tablespoon of pork batter. Cook for 3 minutes, until golden brown.

SAVORY SAUSAGE BREAD

Makes 24 pops

1 tablespoon olive oil

2 cloves garlic, minced

½ pound ground sausage

½ tablespoon crushed red pepper flakes (optional)

1 cup shredded mozzarella cheese

2 tablespoons grated Parmesan cheese

1 recipe Savory Bites Bread Dough (page 91)

marinara sauce or other red sauce, to serve

1. Warm the olive oil in a large skillet over medium heat, then add the garlic. Cook for 1 minute, then add the sausage and red pepper flakes, if using. Cook for about 8 minutes, until the sausage is no longer pink, breaking the meat up with a fork. Line a large plate with 2 paper towels and transfer the cooked sausage onto the plate to drain the oil. Then transfer the sausage meat to a medium bowl. Add the mozzarella and Parmesan cheeses and stir to combine.

2. Divide the dough into 24 (2-inch) squares. Use a mini rolling pin to roll out each square so it's 3 to 4 inches. Fill each square with ½ tablespoon of meat mixture. Pinch the ends of the dough together to close.

3. When the cake pop maker is hot, spray with olive oil. Place 1 dough ball in each well and cook for 2 to 3 minutes, until golden brown. Serve with your favorite marinara or other red sauce.

LAMB, SPINACH, AND FETA MEATBALLS

These are so superquick and easy, and the taste is dramatic. Serve these at a party with toothpicks for easy pickins, or for a nice family dinner.   *Makes 30 pops*

1 (6-ounce) bag steam-in-bag baby spinach

1 pound ground lamb

2 cloves garlic, minced

½ cup panko breadcrumbs

6 ounces feta cheese, crumbled

2 large eggs

salt and pepper

1. Microwave the spinach according to the directions on the bag. Shred the spinach and allow to cool. In a medium bowl, combine the lamb, garlic, breadcrumbs, cheese, eggs, and shredded spinach, and season with salt and pepper.

2. Roll the meat mixture into 1¼-inch balls. If you have a 1¼ tablespoon–capacity cookie scoop, this helps. When the cake pop maker is hot, place 1 meatball in each well and cook for 7 to 8 minutes, until golden brown. Use a paper towel to dab any grease from the cake pop maker in between batches.

VEGETARIAN

GRILLED CHEESE FOR KIDS

If you're not vegetarian, these are very tasty with a ¾-inch piece of cooked bacon (from about 5 slices total) on top of the cheese.   *Makes 20 pops*

1 (7.5-ounce) tube home-style biscuits

10 slices American cheese

1. Cut each biscuit in half for a total of 20, then roll each one out with a mini rolling pin to about ¼ inch thick. Cut your cheese slices in half, then roll up each half into a cheese log.

2. Place 1 cheese log onto each rolled-out biscuit. Wrap the dough over the cheese and pinch the ends closed. Give it a little squish so you have more of a ball instead of a log. Repeat with the remaining ingredients.

3. When the cake pop maker is hot, spray with sunflower or vegetable oil. Place 1 dough ball in each well and cook for 3 minutes, until medium golden brown. Let cool 5 minutes before serving.

PEANUT BUTTER AND JELLY POPS FOR KIDS

These are perfect for your kids' lunch boxes. All the kids will want these!

Makes 20 pops

1 (7.5-ounce) tube home-style biscuits

6 tablespoons plus 2 teaspoons peanut butter (1 teaspoon per pop)

20 teaspoons your favorite preserves

1. Cut each biscuit in half, then roll out each half with a mini rolling pin. Put ½ tablespoon peanut butter and 1 teaspoon preserves onto each rolled-out biscuit. Pinch the ends closed over the filling to form a ball.

2. When the cake pop maker is hot, spray with sunflower or vegetable oil. Place 1 dough ball in each well and cook for 3 minutes until golden brown. Let cool before serving.

BEAN AND PEPPER JACK QUESADILLAS

You can substitute Monterey Jack cheese for the pepper Jack if you don't want your quesadillas to be too spicy, and especially if you want the kids to eat them.   *Makes 48 pops*

FILLING

1 fresh corn on the cob, husk intact

1 tablespoon olive oil

½ medium sweet white onion, diced

1 (15.5-ounce) ounce can black beans, drained and rinsed

1 tablespoon brown sugar

½ teaspoon crushed red pepper flakes

8 ounces pepper Jack cheese, divided into 48 pieces

sour cream, salsa, and guacamole, to serve

DOUGH

3 cups all-purpose flour

1 teaspoon salt

¼ cup vegetable oil

2 tablespoons taco seasoning

1 cup water

1. Prepare the Filling: Microwave the corn cob with the husk on for 3½ minutes on high power. Heat the olive oil in a large sauté pan or skillet over medium heat. Stir in the onion and cook until softened, about 2 minutes. Stir in the black beans and cut the corn off the cob directly into the pan. Finally, add the sugar and red pepper flakes. Stir to combine and cook for another 3 minutes. Then set aside to cool while you make the dough.

2. Prepare the Dough: In a food processor fitted with the metal blade, combine the flour, salt, vegetable oil, and taco seasoning. Pulse to mix and slowly add up to 1 cup of the water until the dough comes together to form a ball.

3. Pinch 1-inch balls from the dough. I got about 48. It's important that all your pieces are about the same size. I make all my dough balls before I fill them. If you are not sure if yours are the right size, then go ahead and fill 1 and cook it, before you prepare all 48. You should get a perfect round pop with no overflow. After you have all your dough balls the right size, use your thumbs to flatten the dough and make a little well to fill. Add a piece of cheese and

1 tablespoon of the bean and corn mixture. Pinch the ends of the dough closed over the mixture. Set aside until all are filled.

4. When the cake pop maker is hot, spray with vegetable oil. Place a dough ball in each well and cook for 4½ minutes, until golden brown. Let cool before eating. Serve with sour cream, salsa, and guacamole.

SPINACH PIE POPS

This makes a complete meal if you pair it with grilled chicken breasts, or add two grilled diced chicken breasts to the mixture for dinner on the go! *Makes 24 pops*

½ medium sweet white onion

2 cloves garlic

2 tablespoons extra-virgin olive oil

5 ounces baby spinach

1 large egg

⅓ cup ricotta cheese

¾ cup crumbled feta cheese

1 (8-ounce) tube seamless crescent dough

1. In a food processor, pulse together the onion and garlic until finely minced. In a large sauté pan or skillet, warm 2 tablespoons of extra-virgin olive oil over medium heat. Add the onion-garlic mixture to the pan and cook for 2 to 3 minutes, until golden brown. Add the spinach leaves and cover the pan with a lid. Turn off the stove and wait 5 minutes for the spinach leaves to steam.

2. Meanwhile, in a large bowl, beat together the egg and ricotta and feta cheeses. Remove the lid from the pan and use a fork and knife to shred the steamed spinach leaves into pieces. Line a large dinner plate with 2 paper towels and transfer the spinach mixture onto the plate to drain. Once cooled, add the spinach to the cheese mixture and stir to combine all ingredients.

3. Roll out the crescent dough and divide into 24 (2-inch) squares. Using a mini rolling pin, roll out each square and fill with 1 tablespoon of the mixture. Pinch the ends of the dough together over the mixture. When the cake pop maker is hot, place 1 dough ball in each well and cook 4 minutes, until medium golden brown.

EGGPLANT PARM BITES

These are great for any occasion. You can substitute the eggplant with three thinly sliced chicken cutlets. Instead of using crescent dough, you can make a batch of Savory Bites Bread Dough (page 91) for this recipe.   *Makes 24 pops*

1 medium eggplant (3½ inches in diameter)

salt

2 eggs

1 tablespoon whole milk

1 cup Italian-style breadcrumbs

¼ cup plus ½ teaspoon olive oil

1 clove garlic

1¼ cups tomato sauce

2 teaspoons parsley flakes

1 fresh basil leaf, shredded

pinch of crushed red pepper flakes

½ cup grated Parmesan cheese

¼ cup shredded mozzarella cheese

1 (8-ounce) tube seamless crescent dough

1. Slice the eggplant into 6 (½-inch-thick) rounds. Sprinkle one side with salt. In a small bowl, beat the eggs with the milk. Measure 1 cup of breadcrumbs onto a small plate. In a large sauté pan or skillet over medium heat, warm ¼ cup of the olive oil. Now, bathe the eggplant section in the egg mixture and then dredge in the breadcrumbs, so that both sides are crumb-covered. Then place the crumb-covered eggplant into the hot oil. Repeat with other eggplant rounds. Turn the heat to low if the eggplant begins to get too dark. Cook for about 5 minutes on each side, then remove the pan from the heat and cover with a lid. This will allow the eggplant to get a little softer.

2. In a small saucepan over medium heat, warm the remaining ½ teaspoon olive oil and sauté the garlic for 1 minute. Then add the red sauce, parsley, basil, and red pepper flakes. Cook the sauce for about 7 minutes, stirring occasionally. Next, season the sauce with a little salt and pepper if needed. Remove from the heat and add the Parmesan and mozzarella cheeses to the red sauce. Remove the eggplant pieces from the pan and set on a paper towel to soak up any excess oil.

3. Cut the eggplant again into ½-inch-square pieces, almost as if you were dicing it. Each round section will fill 4 pops. Roll out the crescent dough and divide into 24 (2-inch) squares. Using a mini rolling pin, roll out each square and fill with about 5 pieces

of eggplant. Top it off with 1 teaspoon of cheese sauce. Pinch the ends of the dough closed over the eggplant and sauce filling.

4. When the cake pop maker is hot, add 1 dough ball to each well. Cook for 3 minutes, until golden brown. Allow the pops to cool for a few minutes before serving.

MAC AND CHEESE POPS

Makes 30 pops

2½ tablespoons sweet cream butter

5½ tablespoons all-purpose flour

¾ cup whole milk

¼ cup light cream

½ teaspoon Dijon mustard

1 teaspoon salt

freshly ground black pepper

¼ teaspoon crushed red pepper flakes

½ cup shredded Gruyère or Swiss cheese

½ cup shredded cheddar cheese

½ pound elbow macaroni, cooked

1 cup panko breadcrumbs

½ cup grated Parmesan cheese

2 large eggs

1. Melt the butter in a large saucepan over medium-high heat. Add the flour and cook for 2 minutes, whisking, being sure to get all the lumps out. Pour in the milk and light cream, and when it comes to a boil, reduce the heat to low and let it simmer for about 5 minutes, stirring. Then, add the Dijon mustard, salt, fresh black pepper, and red pepper flakes. Sprinkle in the Gruyère or Swiss cheese and the cheddar cheese. Whisk until smooth and remove from the heat. Add the cheese mixture to the cooked elbow pasta. Taste and season with salt if needed. Allow the pasta and cheese mixture to cool for about 5 minutes.

2. On a large plate, combine the breadcrumbs and Parmesan cheese. When the pasta and cheese mixture is somewhat cool, add the 2 eggs and combine gently.

3. Using a 1½-tablespoon scoop, or a heaping tablespoon, scoop pasta into your palm. Using the opposite hand, sprinkle with the breadcrumb mixture. Then switch the pasta mixture into your other hand and sprinkle again with breadcrumbs. Place in a mound on waxed paper and continue with the remaining ingredients.

4. When the cake pop maker is hot, spray with olive oil. Gently place 1 pasta mound in each well and cook for 4 minutes, until light to medium golden brown. Gently the remove pops with a small spoon.

TRUFFLED MAC AND CHEESE: Drizzle 1 to 2 teaspoons white truffle oil onto the pasta before adding the cheese mixture.

SPICY MAC AND CHEESE: Omit the Gruyère or Swiss cheese, and replace with 1 cup shredded pepper Jack cheese.

BASIL-MOZZARELLA CHEESE POPS WITH BALSAMIC DRIZZLE

Toschi Balmi Balsamic Glaze is a must-have in the kitchen. It tastes great on almost anything, but it's my favorite on fried calamari. Balmi Glaze is available on Amazon.com.   *Makes 24 pops*

4 ounces mozzarella cheese

⅓ cup finely chopped fresh basil

1 (8-ounce) tube seamless crescent dough

2 tablespoons balsamic vinegar glaze, like Toschi Balmi brand

1. Cut the cheese into 1-inch squares. Toss the cheese and chopped basil together. For a strong basil flavor, refrigerate overnight.

2. Roll out the crescent dough and divide into 24 (2-inch) squares. Using a mini rolling pin, roll each dough square out and fill with 1 basil-cheese square (at this point they should be stuck together). Pinch the opposite ends of the dough over the filling to form a ball.

3. When the cake pop maker is hot, place 1 dough ball in each well. Cook for 4 minutes, until golden brown. Arrange the pops on a plate to cool and drizzle with a zigzag of the balsamic vinegar glaze, if using.

BAKED BRIE

Makes 24 pops

½ pound double-cream Brie, rind removed

1 (8-ounce) tube seamless crescent dough

½ cup seedless raspberry preserves

1. Cut the Brie into 24 (1 x ½-inch) pieces.

2. Roll out the crescent dough and divide into 24 (2-inch) squares.

3. Using your mini rolling pin, roll out each square and scoop ¼ teaspoon of the preserves onto the dough, and then top with a piece of Brie. Pinch the opposite ends of the dough together and form a ball.

4. When the cake pop maker is hot, place 1 dough ball in each well and cook for 3 minutes, until golden brown. Serve slightly warm or at room temperature.

EASY SPINACH AND ARTICHOKE CHEESE POPS

Makes 18 pops

1 (8-ounce) box frozen spinach and artichoke cheese dip

1 tablespoon grated Parmesan cheese

1 recipe Savory Bites Bread Dough (page 91)

1. Warm the cheese dip according to the directions on the box, but cook it 1 minute less than indicated since it will be warmed again in the cake pop maker. Add the Parmesan cheese to the dip and stir to combine.

2. Roll out the bread dough and divide into 24 (2-inch) squares (you'll only need 18 for this recipe). Using a mini rolling pin, roll each square out so it's 3 to 4 inches and fill with ½ tablespoon of dip. Pinch the dough ends together over the spinach-cheese dip.

3. When the cake pop maker is hot, spray with olive oil. Place 1 dough ball in each well and cook for 3 minutes, until golden brown. These will be very hot. Allow to cool 5 minutes before serving.

BROCCOLI AND CHEESE BITES

Makes 48 pops

2 cups frozen broccoli florets, steamed

2 large eggs

1 cup whole milk

2 tablespoons sweet cream butter, melted

1 teaspoon Worcestershire sauce

1 teaspoon Dijon mustard

1 cup all-purpose flour

½ teaspoon kosher salt

3 tablespoons grated Parmesan cheese

1 teaspoon baking powder

¼ cup finely chopped sweet white onions

1 cup shredded cheddar cheese

salt and pepper

1. In food processer or blender, pulse the steamed broccoli until finely chopped, but not pureed. Transfer the broccoli to a small bowl. Then, in the same processer or blender, pulse or blend the eggs, milk, butter, Worcestershire sauce, and Dijon mustard. Next, add the flour, salt, Parmesan cheese, and baking powder to the food processor blender, and pulse or blend until combined. Transfer to a large bowl.

2. Add the broccoli, onions, and cheese to the batter. Season with salt and pepper before stirring to combine.

3. When the cake pop maker is hot, spray with sunflower or vegetable oil. Scoop 1 heaping tablespoon of the mixture into each well. Cook for 4 minutes, until dark brown in spots. Enjoy hot or warm.

BLACK BEAN BITES

Makes 30 pops

1 (15.5-ounce) can black beans, drained and rinsed

2 cloves garlic

½ teaspoon crushed red pepper flakes

1 medium red onion

handful of fresh cilantro

1 large tomato

2 tablespoons balsamic vinegar

salt

1 recipe Savory Bites Bread Dough (page 91)

1. Combine the black beans, garlic, and red pepper flakes in a food processor. Process for about 2 minutes until smooth. Transfer to a medium bowl.

2. Finely chop the red onion and shred the cilantro. Seed and dice the tomato. Mix these ingredients together in a second medium bowl, sprinkle with salt, and drizzle with the balsamic vinegar.

3. Roll out the dough to a 10 x 12-inch rectangle and divide into 30 squares (the squares will be a little smaller than 1¾ inches). Using a mini rolling pin, roll out each square. Onto each square, scoop ½ tablespoon bean puree and 1 teaspoon tomato mixture. Pinch the ends of the dough closed over the filling.

4. When the cake pop maker is hot, place 1 dough ball seam side up (this will minimize any filling from leaking out) in each well and cook for 2½ minutes, until golden brown.

BLACK BEAN-CHEDDAR BITES: Omit the tomato mixture and instead sprinkle 1 teaspoon shredded cheddar cheese on top of the bean puree in each pop.

SAVORY BITES BREAD DOUGH

Makes dough for 48 pops

1¼ cups warm water

1½ tablespoons sugar

1 (¼-ounce) packet active dry yeast

1½ teaspoons kosher salt

3 cups all-purpose flour

1 tablespoon olive oil

½ teaspoon baking powder

1. In a food processor, pulse together the water, sugar, and yeast. Remove the blade and let sit for 5 minutes. Then, replace the blade and add the salt, flour, oil, and baking powder. Process until a ball of dough forms.

2. Cut the dough ball in half. On parchment paper, roll out each half separately into an 8 x 12-inch rectangle. Cover the dough with a piece of plastic wrap and allow to sit for 30 minutes before using.

3. To divide the bread dough to use in a recipe, cut a rectangle of dough into 2-inch squares, enough for 24 pops per rectangle. Some recipes in this book yield more than 24 pops, and this bread can be divided differently to fit those recipes. To save uncooked dough, after you roll the dough into a rectangle, roll it up in parchment paper like a log and twist the ends of the paper. This will help retain moisture and will make preparation much easier when you're ready to use it. Store unused dough in the refrigerator.

4. To make Savory Bread Pops, when the cake pop maker is hot, spray lightly with olive oil. Roll each dough square into a ball, and place a ball in each well. Cook for 2 minutes, until golden brown.

CRANBERRY, GOAT CHEESE, AND CARAMELIZED ONION POPS

Makes 24 pops

1 tablespoon olive oil

1 large sweet onion, finely chopped

1 teaspoon sugar

1 recipe Savory Bites Bread Dough
(page 91)

3½ ounces goat cheese, crumbled

1 (14-ounce) can whole-berry cranberry
sauce

1. In a medium sauté pan or skillet over medium heat, warm the olive oil. Add the chopped onion and sugar and cook until the onions are caramelized, about 8 minutes, stirring every so often so they do not burn. Allow to cool while preparing the dough.

2. Roll out the dough and divide into 24 (2-inch) squares Using the mini rolling pin, roll out each square to 3 to 4 inches, about ⅛ inch thick. In the center of each dough square, place 1 teaspoon crumbled goat cheese, ½ teaspoon cranberry sauce, and ½ teaspoon caramelized onion. Pinch opposite ends of the dough together over the filling to form a ball.

3. When the cake pop maker is hot, spray with sunflower or vegetable oil. Place 1 dough ball in each well and cook for 3 minutes, until lightly golden brown.

DESSERT

SINFUL CHEESECAKE BITES

Makes 24 pops

8 ounces cream cheese

⅓ cup sugar

½ teaspoon vanilla extract

3 (2.07-ounce) Snickers bars

2 (8-ounce) tubes seamless crescent dough

1. In a medium bowl, stir together the cream cheese, sugar, and vanilla. Cut each Snickers bar into 10 equal pieces.

2. Roll out the crescent dough and divide each sheet into 12 equal squares. Roll out each square with a mini rolling pin. Spoon 1 teaspoon of cream cheese mixture onto each dough square. Put 1 Snickers piece on top of the cream cheese. Pinch opposite ends of the dough together over the mixture to form a ball.

3. When the cake pop maker is hot, place 1 dough ball in each well. Cook for 3 minutes, until golden brown. Let cool before serving.

RASPBERRY-CHEESE DANISH POPS WITH LEMON DRIZZLE

Makes 24 pops

1 recipe Savory Bites Bread Dough (page 91)

6 ounces cream cheese

1 (12-ounce) can raspberry cake and pie filling

1 cup powdered sugar

1½ tablespoons fresh lemon juice

½ tablespoon whole milk

1. Roll out the dough and cut into 24 (2-inch) squares. Using a mini rolling pin, roll out each of the squares so it's 3 to 4 inches. Place ½ tablespoon of cream cheese and 1 teaspoon of the raspberry filling on top of each dough square. Pinch the ends of the dough together over the filling.

2. In a small bowl, mix together the powdered sugar and lemon juice. Add the milk and whisk together. Set aside.

3. When the cake pop maker is hot, place 1 dough ball in each well and cook for 2½ minutes, until golden brown. Let cool for 2 minutes. Arrange the pops on a serving plate and slowly pour the lemon drizzle over the top in a zigzag motion. Serve warm!

SWEET POTATO PIE

This recipe calls for fresh sweet potato, but if you don't have time to follow the made-from-scratch method, you can easily cheat with a simple step. Rather than cooking a fresh sweet potato and mixing it with spices, you can use sweet potato casserole as pie filling. I like to get a container from Boston Market, but some grocery stores sell it in the frozen section. *Makes 16 pops*

1 extra-large sweet potato (about ¾ pound), peeled and cooked

¼ cup granulated sugar

¼ cup brown sugar

½ teaspoon vanilla extract

¼ teaspoon ground cinnamon

¼ teaspoon ground nutmeg

2 tablespoons sweet cream butter

1 teaspoon maple syrup

1 large egg

prepared dough for 1 (9-inch) pie crust

1. Combine all the ingredients except the pie dough in a large bowl and mix until smooth.

2. Unroll the pie dough from its package and cut into 16 (2-inch) squares. Spoon 1¼ tablespoons of filling onto each dough square. Pinch the opposite ends of the dough over the filling to close.

3. When the cake pop maker is hot, spray with sunflower or vegetable oil. Cook for 7 minutes, until golden brown. Serve warm.

APPLE PIE BITES

To serve these bites at the end of an intimate dinner with family or friends, place a bite on top of a scoop of vanilla ice cream. Drizzle with hot chocolate syrup!   *Makes 24 pops*

¼ cup (½ stick) sweet cream butter, at room temperature

¼ teaspoon ground cinnamon

2 tablespoons brown sugar

1 large Granny Smith apple

¼ teaspoon pure vanilla extract

prepared dough for 1 (9-inch) pie

1. In a small bowl, cream together the butter, cinnamon, and brown sugar. Peel the apple and cut into quarters. Cut out the seeds, then slice each quarter horizontally and then diagonally. You'll have 16 pieces of apple altogether. Drizzle the vanilla over the apple pieces.

2. Roll out the pie dough and divide it into 16 (2-inch) squares. Using your mini rolling pin, roll out each dough square enough to accommodate the filling, about 3½ inches. Spread ¼ teaspoon of the butter and sugar mixture onto the center of each dough square and then place 1 apple piece on top. Close the opposite ends of the dough together over the filling and pinch to seal.

3. When the cake pop maker is hot, spray with sunflower or vegetable oil. Place 1 dough ball in each well and cook for 7 minutes, until golden brown.

S'MORES POPS

These are great to serve on lollipop or wooden sticks. Simply insert the stick while the pop is hot, then let cool for 5 minutes. *Makes 30 pops*

DOUGH

2½ cups all-purpose flour

¾ cup dark brown sugar

1 teaspoon ground cinnamon

1 teaspoon baking soda

½ cup (1 stick) sweet cream butter

⅓ cup honey

¼ cup whole milk

1 tablespoon vanilla extract

FILLING

1 (16-ounce bag) mini marshmallows

2 (8-count) packs Hershey's mini snack size chocolate bars

1. Prepare the Dough: In a food processor, combine the flour, sugar, cinnamon, and baking soda, and process to combine. Then add the butter and pulse until combined. In a small bowl, combine the honey, milk, and vanilla. Add the liquids to the flour mixture. Pulse until the dough comes together and forms a soft ball. Turn the dough out onto a large piece of parchment paper. Wrap the paper around the dough to seal. Refrigerate for at least an hour.

2. Unroll the parchment and pinch off about a 1-inch ball of dough. Flatten the dough ball with your thumbs and make a well. Insert 3 mini marshmallows and 1 piece of a mini chocolate bar into the well. Wrap the dough over the filling and roll into a ball. Be sure none of the filling is exposed. If it is, gently push it back inside the dough.

3. When the cake pop maker is hot, place 1 dough ball in each well and cook for 2 minutes, until light golden brown.

HOT COCOA KRISPIES COOKIES

Makes 40 pops

1 cup (2 sticks) sweet cream butter, at room temperature

1 cup sugar

2 (1.25-ounce) packets hot cocoa mix

1 large egg

1/2 teaspoon vanilla extract

2¾ cups all-purpose flour

1 teaspoon baking soda

1/2 teaspoon baking powder

5 (.78-ounce) individually wrapped Rice Krispies Treat bars

1. Cream together the butter, sugar, and hot cocoa mix until smooth, and then beat in the egg and the vanilla. Next, add the flour, baking soda, and baking powder. Mix until the dough is well combined.

2. Cut the Rice Krispies Treats into 8 segments per bar. Pinch an inch of the dough and make a well in the middle of the dough piece to put 1 Rice Krispies segment. Wrap the dough around the Krispie to enclose it in the middle. Repeat this until all the Krispies are wrapped in dough. There should be 40 dough balls.

3. When the cake pop maker is hot, place 1 dough ball in each of 10 wells. Cook each batch for 4 minutes and then remove. Let cool completely before serving.

CHOCOLATE CHIP COOKIE BROWNIE CUPCAKES

You will have leftover brownie batter from this recipe. You can use the extra batter to try other variations of these pops. Instead of filling the batter with cookie dough, try miniature Reese's Peanut Butter Cups, mini marshmallows, caramel pieces, nuts, or candy bar pieces that are about ¼ inch long.   *Makes 12 cupcakes*

1 (8-ounce) box Jiffy Fudge Brownie Mix

1 tablespoon water

2 tablespoons vegetable oil

8 ounces prepared chocolate cookie dough

1 (9-ounce) box Jiffy Golden Yellow Cake Mix

2 large eggs, divided

½ cup cold water

8 ounces chocolate or strawberry frosting

1. In a medium bowl, stir together the brownie mix, 1 tablespoon water, and vegetable oil. Next, cut the cookie dough into ¼-inch squares. You will need 12.

2. When the your cake pop maker is hot, use a ½-tablespoon measure to spoon ½ tablespoon of brownie mix into each well, then quickly add a piece of cookie dough, and then top it with ½ tablespoon more of brownie mix. Repeat until 6 wells are filled. Then cook for 8 minutes, until the pops are fully expanded and slightly browned. Remove using the fork included with the cake pop maker. Repeat with the remaining batter and cookie dough.

3. Preheat the oven to 350°F. In another medium bowl, combine the cake mix, eggs, and cold water with an electric mixer or 300 strokes if stirring by hand. Line a standard 12-cup cupcake pan with paper liners. Fill each of the liners about one-fourth full with cake batter, then quickly add a cake pop, then top with one-fourth more cake batter. Bake cupcakes for about 17 minutes, until golden brown. Let cool, then frost the cupcakes with chocolate or strawberry frosting (or your favorite flavor).

CHOCOLATE WALNUT STRUDEL

Makes 24 pops

½ cup mini semisweet chocolate chips

4 ounces walnuts, pulsed in food processer

2 (8-ounce) tubes seamless crescent dough

powdered sugar, for sprinkling (optional)

1. In a small bowl, combine the chocolate chips and walnuts.

2. Roll out the crescent dough and divide each sheet into 12 equal squares. Roll out each square with a mini rolling pin and sprinkle with the chocolate and nut mixture. Roll each piece of dough into a log and pinch the ends together.

3. When the cake pop maker is hot, place 1 dough ball in each well and cook for 3 minutes, until golden brown. Let cool a few minutes, then sprinkle with powdered sugar, if using, to serve.

LAVA POPS WITH VANILLA ICE CREAM AND RASPBERRY DRIZZLE

These are the perfect ending to a special meal, and they can be prepared very quickly. *Makes 8 pops*

¼ cup (½ stick) sweet cream butter

2 ounces bittersweet chocolate

1 large egg

1 large egg yolk

¼ teaspoon vanilla extract

3 tablespoons sugar

1½ tablespoons all-purpose flour

½ gallon vanilla ice cream

½ cup raspberry or strawberry preserves

1. In a small microwave-safe bowl, combine the butter and chocolate and microwave until melted and smooth, about 1½ minutes on high power. Then transfer to a medium bowl and add the egg, egg yolk, vanilla, sugar, and flour. Whisk to combine. The batter should look a bit like pudding; if not, let it sit for a minute or 2 to set up.

2. Scoop large scoops of ice cream into a dish or bowl, one scoop for each person. Using a spoon, make a well on top of each scoop by removing a small portion off the top of the ice cream. Keep the scoops in the freezer until ready to serve. Next, microwave the raspberry or strawberry preserves until melted, about 45 seconds on high power. I use a glass measuring cup to make it easy to drizzle.

3. When the cake pop maker is hot, fill each well with a heaping tablespoon of the batter. Cook for 4 minutes, until medium golden brown. Place 1 pop on top of each ice cream scoop. Drizzle the raspberry sauce back and forth over the top. Serve while the pop is warm.

FRIED ICE CREAM

These are by far my favorite special occasion dessert. They are a bit difficult the first time around, but once you get the hang of it, the flavor is well worth it!

Makes 16 pops

3 cups cornflakes

1½ teaspoons ground cinnamon

3 tablespoons sweet cream butter

3 large eggs

1 tablespoon warm honey

1 gallon vanilla ice cream

chocolate syrup, for drizzling

1. In a food processor, pulse together the cornflakes, cinnamon, and butter. Transfer the crumbs to a medium bowl. In a separate bowl, beat together the eggs and honey. Prepare a plate in the freezer to put the crumb-and-egg-dipped ice cream balls on.

2. Scoop a generous ½ tablespoon of ice cream, then lightly roll the ice cream scoop in the crumb mixture. It should not be too thick or completely covered. Now dip the ball into the egg and honey bath, and then back into the crumb mixture. It should not be wider than a tablespoon-sized ball, since it will need to fit into the cake pop well. Immediately put the ball directly onto the plate in the freezer. Repeat with the remaining ingredients. Leave in freezer overnight or for at least a couple of hours.

3. When the ice cream balls are frozen and the cake pop maker is hot, get the chocolate syrup ready to drizzle. I like to cook 4 ice cream balls at a time. Place 1 ice cream ball in each of 4 wells and cook until the "ready" light goes out, almost 1 minute. Remove the pops, drizzle with chocolate syrup, and serve immediately. Repeat with the remaining ice cream balls.

CONVERSIONS

Useful Conversions

U.S. MEASURE	EQUIVALENT		METRIC
1 teaspoon	--		5 milliliters
1 tablespoon	3 teaspoons		15 milliliters
1 cup	16 tablespoons		240 milliliters
1 pint	2 cups		470 milliliters
1 quart	4 cups		950 milliliters
1 liter	4 cups + 3½ tablespoons		1000 milliliters
1 ounce (dry)	2 tablespoons		28 grams
1 pound	16 ounces		450 grams
2.21 pounds	35.3 ounces		1 kilogram
270°F / 350°F	--		132°C / 177°C

Volume Conversions

U.S. MEASURE	EQUIVALENT	METRIC
(3 teaspoons)	1 tablespoon, ½ fluid ounce	15 milliliters
¼ cup	2 fluid ounces	60 milliliters
⅓ cup	3 fluid ounces	90 milliliters
½ cup	4 fluid ounces	120 milliliters
⅔ cup	5 fluid ounces	150 milliliters
¾ cup	6 fluid ounces	180 milliliters
1 cup	8 fluid ounces	240 milliliters
2 cups	16 fluid ounces	480 milliliters

Weight Conversions

U.S. MEASURE	METRIC
½ ounce	15 grams
1 ounce	30 grams
2 ounces	60 grams
¼ pound	115 grams
⅓ pound	150 grams
½ pound	225 grams
¾ pound	350 grams
1 pound	450 grams

INDEX

ACKNOWLEDGMENTS

I would like to thank my husband, Vinny, and daughter, Emily, for being so patient with me while cooking. For the love they give and for being my guinea pigs.

For my bestest friend ever, Kaye Taylor, not only for being my main source of encouragement, but for always believing that if I say I'm going to do something, I will.

I would like to thank my sisters, Shawn, Shannon, Amy, and Jen, for being in my life, and also my mother, who has always been there.

Above all, thank you to God, for making me special and wonderful in His image. This always makes me feel beautiful, and I know that through Him all things are possible.

Thank you to the staff at Ulysses Press, for believing in me and my ideas for this book. Especially Kelly and Lauren, for all their assistance in putting it together.

ABOUT THE AUTHOR

Heather Torrone was born and raised in New Jersey, where she lives with her husband and daughter. She has always enjoyed cooking, and takes classes at New York Institute for Culinary Education during her free time. Since the cake pop maker came out, it has been her true passion to cook and invent recipes for the appliance. Upon completion of this book, she has begun catering events for close family and friends with savory bites. She hopes to turn this passion into a full-time catering business.